Satellite Convulsions

Satellite

Poems from *Tin House*

Convulsions

TinHouseBooks

Published by Tin House Books, Portland, Oregon, and New York, New York

Distributed to the trade by Publishers Group West, 1700 Fourth St., Berkeley, CA 94710, www.pgw.com

ISBN 10: 0-9794198-9-1
ISBN 13: 978-0-9794198-9-8

First U.S. edition 2008
Interior design by Laura Shaw Design, Inc.

Printed in Canada

www.tinhouse.com

CONTENTS

FOREWORD

Tin House began ten years ago with the idea that a literary magazine doesn't have to be staid: it can look good; it can be non- (or even un-) academic; it can wear its politics on its sleeve, chest, and forehead; and it can reach and be enjoyed by a mass audience. As part of the pursuit of that mass audience, *Tin House* should have jettisoned poetry from its pages long ago in favor of more fiction or—even better—pictures of some scantily clad youth.

But at *Tin House* we like to break rules, especially the rule that says a magazine is better served in the twenty-first century without poetry. Instead, we believe that poetry doesn't have to be stodgy, academic, elitist, my-mommy-didn't-love me crap. Poetry can be as sexy as any scantily clad youth, as gritty as war reportage, as grim as the best fake memoir. We don't care about the argument of whether poetry is dead or not. We don't care about schools or who dubs whom what. We care about the ability of a poem to leave us changed at the break of every line.

When I first began working at *Tin House* in the Portland office as a wide-eyed wannabe, the poetry editor was the kind but commanding disembodied voice of Amy Bartlett coming over the speakerphone during our weekly editorial meetings. I was fresh off the boat from nowheresville and, though my time with her was too too brief, Amy taught me that editors argue for a poem they want to publish, and if you can't fight for it until you're fully pink-faced and clammy, you don't really believe in it. So we argued, read poems both great and mediocre, and then argued some more.

Then, one day in 2004, that voice was missing from the meeting, and then the following meeting. Amy Bartlett died of cancer not long after, and while *Tin House* lost an editor and friend, we all lost an amazing poet—full of leap, surprise, and the most wicked truth, as her poems in this anthology illustrate. Luckily for us all, editors and readers alike, Brenda Shaughnessy yielded to our clumsy advances and agreed to join our little cabal, bringing her editorial deftness, ferocious wit, and the determination to publish more up-and-coming poets alongside the heavy hitters.

In addition to the familiar names, in every issue of *Tin House* we publish new voices, writers with little, if not no, previous publishing experience. We search high and low (and in the ever-growing pile of slush) for these young savants. And in every issue we actually *feature* poems—only fifteen or so pages of the very best we can find. Ever the exhibitionists, we bare ourselves and our poets, saying, "Here is what we like. Judge it, judge us, but expect no apologies for our eccentricities."

Ultimately, all we ask for is poems that rub us raw and then invite us back for another go-round. The ones that leave us feeling that, as Ben Doller writes in the poem that lends its title to this anthology, "There must be this wire shaking / loose in my mind, an unattended firehose, a spasmodic / filament attempting to cool the baby planet but lacerating / precious gray matter."

Rereading these poems, I'm reminded of the quickened pulse and dilated pupils that came with slicing open the envelopes and seeing them for the first time. Hopefully you too, gentle reader, will enjoy the view—sometimes terrible, sometimes jubilant, sometimes lovingly pocked and scarred. Pour a martini, settle in, and prepare to be changed at the break of every line.

—CJ Evans

INTRODUCTION

"A mysterious power that all may feel and no philosophy can explain."

—GOETHE (as quoted by Federico García Lorca
in his essay "The Duende: Theory and Divertissement")

I.

I recall an early conversation I had with *Tin House* magazine publisher and editor in chief Win McCormack concerning the notion that poetry is "ineffable" and that this is one of its most transformative—and confounding—qualities. Of course, ineffability is by definition a linguistic conundrum, meaning, as it does, "inexpressible" and "unutterable." Yet the word and its collection of meanings exist. Poets understand this existential, linguistic doubleness: we express the inexpressible through poetry, thereby rendering the inexpressible no longer so. Abstract subjectivity becomes a textual object, a real thing. Yet this "real thing's" elusive essence remains, because it is the reader's subjectivity that makes it real. And that subjectivity is, one might say, ineffable.

This quality in poetry has been named in several ways: Keats's "negative capability" notes the endless psychic space that may be accessed in poetry, and Lorca defines the notion of the *duende*, a spirit or a dark power infusing mere words on paper with a kind of mysterious life blood.

As a political writer and intellectual, Win cares about clarity. As a magazine publisher and editor, he cares about readability. He asked the reasonable, even charming, question: "But can't poetry also be effable?"

One would think, given the way I've set up this scenario, that clarity/readability lives in opposition to the ineffable. But in fact, the poets published in *Tin House* make a strong case for the possibility that both can exist under one roof. The poets in *Satellite Convulsions: Poems from Tin House* exhibit various sorts of genius, and if any general rubric can be said to unite them it is this: these minds make themselves known, clearly, darkly, wildly, mysteriously. By what means this knowledge is imparted, how these poets' minds travel all the way to our own . . . well, if I knew that, I'd be an advanced third-year sorcery resident instead of entering my fifth year as poetry editor. And yet a kind of sorcery is always at work when poetry is put forth in the world.

II.

It is a strange tribe gathered here. What, for example, does the poetic sensibility of Seamus Heaney have in common with that of Matthea Harvey, Cecily Parks, or Bin Ramke? How do the dark powers of Dennis Nurkse or D. A. Powell interact with the klieg light of Jessica Reed? Some of the poets in this collection appeared in the House due solely to the editorial powers of the late poetry editor Amy Bartlett. Amy was responsible for bringing in some of poetry's greatest luminaries, including Yehuda Amichai, Donald Hall, Pablo Neruda, Sharon Olds, Wislawa Szymborska, to name only a few. Other poets, like Charles Simic and Billy Collins, are *Tin House* regulars, having appeared in several issues over the years, throughout both Amy's tenure and my own.

It is always an incredible pleasure to publish poems written by the marvelous poets who've inspired me, my heroes, such as Frank Bidart, Bruce Smith, Lucia Perillo, and Rae Armantrout. And perhaps nothing is more exciting for a poetry editor than finding a genuine New Voice. What a tremendous privilege and pleasure it is to help put into print someone with the talent of Diana Park or Christopher Schmidt. And it is also a true honor to reprint the work of beloved poets who have passed away but whose work will not be forgotten, including Shahid Agha Ali, Amy Bartlett, and Jason Shinder.

In an effort to cover the range of contributors, I seem to have categorized the above-mentioned poets. I hadn't meant to, but sometimes a little order is necessary—if only to see how easily these categories are overrun by their constituents. Donald Hall will not stay neatly in his spot as a "Bartlett-era" *Tin House* poet. He belongs to all of us who read him. And Christopher Schmidt was a New Voice for a hot second before his first book was snapped up this year. None of the poets in this anthology will remain in a category for as long as it takes to finish a paragraph. They are all over the place. And yet they each have a place. *Tin House* publishes the world's most venerable poets in the same issue as brand-new, just-hatched poets, jauntily mixing poets at every point in the continuum; but this isn't the weird part. Many magazines strive for a mix. The weird part is that, very often, *Tin House* offers the galvanizing combination of expectation and surprise: between prose pieces, a Nick Flynn poem pops up—and this is exciting. We (readers, poets, and editors alike) are excited because when we see Nick Flynn's name we know to expect brilliance. It's a reasonable expectation. But then upon reading "Fire" the illumination is all new. We didn't expect to be blown away in quite this way, right? This "all-newness," this sense that we can be surprised repeatedly by a poet whose work we know well, is the kind of thing a reader can expect from *Tin House*.

So am I saying that what makes a poem right for *Tin House* is that it fulfills the expectation of surprise? This seems abstract. How, more plainly, do we know a poem belongs in *Tin House*? I say "we" because CJ Evans, intrepid associate poetry editor, and I are not working alone. All the poems—as well as all the fiction—under consideration for the magazine are vetted through the entire editorial team. It is truly a group or, I should say, "family," effort. Each member of the clan weighs in on whether a poem should be published in the magazine. Though CJ and I like to pretend we have a magic wand with which to wave a spell of agreement among the cacophony, in the end, it is really the strength of the poems, the power of the poets' voices, that makes the decisions for us. From ineffable to inevitable. Talk about *duende*!

III.

Perhaps it's of note that the poet Win and I were speaking of, when we spoke of (in)effability, was Ben Doller, whose poetic style is certainly one of marked psychic complexity. Ben Doller, formerly known as Ben Doyle, was an early *Tin House* New Voice in Issue 5, in the year 2000. One of his poems published in that issue was "Satellite Convulsions," a title that proved evocative enough to become eponymous (from the

Greek: giving name) of the anthology you are reading. The poem is dense, packed with strange utterance and incredible images, the poet's voice alone having the authority and strength necessary to propel the universe of the poem onto the page:

> I keep forgetting
>
> the rules, a Ptolemaniac with stars & suns circling me; I keep
> missing my cues, can't arrange the particles moments are made of—
>
> and it's all good!—because when I bend seriously back & peep
> at the satellite convulsions I am a sluiceway for night rain.

Like the speaker in Doller's poem, I, too, keep forgetting the rules. But the pages of *Tin House* devoted to poetry always remind me that the poet's voice lives on the page and the poem belongs to the one who reads the poem.

When I think about what is utterable I find I cannot define it. When I think about what kind of poem is good, what kind of poem makes a lasting mark, what kind of poem makes real the elusive realities of the imagination, I find that, in the end, the effable is the ineffable, and vice versa. When I read a poem that I cannot entirely suss in a single reading—but which makes my heart race and my explanations die in the air—I believe I am reading some miracle that has managed to fuse the inexpressible with its unlikely but only vehicle: expression. I am reading a poem that transforms the longing for words into art, art into material on the page, and the page into a part of human consciousness. And for this transformation to occur, to quote any old movie involving drag racing: "The rules are, there are no rules."

The best poets are here. Their poems map their way onto the reader's psyche, and in doing so, they've made their own, real worlds. We can partake of these worlds, and while we are there, mute the discussion of ineffability. In fact, I have discussed too much here; it is on the following pages that the real conversation begins. Tin House Books has devoted a wing of rooms to some divine poetry, and the door opens as soon as I shut up. Or, as better expressed in Dennis Nurkse's poem "Parousia": "When we were in the same room as the gods / there was little to say."

—Brenda Shaughnessy

AFTER YOU

We are left mute and so much is left unnamed after you—
No one is left in this world to be blamed after you.

Someone has disappeared after christening Bertha—
Shahid, will a hurricane ever be named after you?

Now from Miami to Boston Bertha is breaking her bones—
I find her in the parking lot. She says, "I'm blamed after you."

The Deluge would happen—it was claimed—after you.
But the world did go on, unashamed, after you.

ANDREW BERTHA CHARLES DAVID ELLA FLOYD GEORGE
    but S comes so late in the alphabet that although
SHAHID DEVASTATES FLORIDA is your dream headline,
    no hurricane will ever be named after you.

YEHUDA AMICHAI

Translated by Chana Bloch and Chana Kronfeld

ALL THE MOTIONS AND POSITIONS

All the motions and the positions in my body—
it's already been done.
I sit on a chair and think like Rodin's Thinker.
Ever since I sat folded up in my mother's belly,
I have carried inside me the wisdom of the folding chair.
My arms are raised like Moses' arms when he raised the Tablets of
   the Law,
my arms are raised without holding a thing,
a bit in disbelief, a bit in despair.
I give hugs like King David on the roof, or helpless hugs
like Jesus on the cross, but the palms of my hands
are free, I am free, though everything
has already come to pass. I have learned to swim
in the stream of consciousness, and I know a thing or two
about the difference between wire and wireless, God and
No-God, jet and chopper, a door
that opens and closes with a slam
and a revolving door that keeps revolving.

Translated by Chana Bloch and Chana Kronfeld

LIFE IS CALLED LIFE

I.

Life is called life as the west wind is called
west, though it blows toward the east.
The way death is called death, though it blows toward life.
In a cemetery we remember the living, and outside it—
the dead. As the past leads to the future
though it's called past, as you to me and I to you in love
though I'm called by my name and you by yours.
As spring provides for summer, as summer beds down into fall.
As my thoughts will be till the end of my life. That is the banner of
    my God.

2.

Each day now I hear the circles of my life closing,
the click of buckles, like kisses
of conciliation and love. And these lend a rhythm
to the final version of my life. Things that were lost long ago
find their places now, like billiard balls, each one into its pocket.
Contracts and prophecies are fulfilled, prophecies true and false.
I come upon the missing lids of pots and pans that stayed uncovered,
I find the matching pieces, like an ancient contract of clay,
broken into two parts, unequal but fitting together.
Like a mosaic, like a jigsaw puzzle, children searching
for the missing pieces. When the game is over,
the picture will be whole. Complete.

STEPHANIE ANDERSON

THE MULE SPINDLES

Are spun-out to threshing, but not threshing.

Dust tracking above thread
or form. Some husking,
dehusking, and you flying shuttle.

The form is watching the field or washing sills.

But then, you already know
how I place. Enacted place. Weft
when it becomes another utterance—

a stone boat stone-full against hill to forest—

to ritual. Or interlaced.
When task was a way
to utter task.

The form watching field against hill to forest.

But then, place becomes
tool when task lacks
tools. The second form,

the form which turns from eye to eaves,

justifies task. You flying shuttle
amidst cues of
dust, stone. My own

husking against change. Staying form's

quivers, I know, and using
cue as tool. The task
of eaves is placed

to track; I like that. Succeeding with tools—

punch cards still
pushed to clocks and trees
carried on trains—

clacking, of course, signals industry; neat

ends. Clean clothes
and other replacements.
Leftover thread or jar.

I horde these ends for use; future impending weft,

knowing that they remain
as husks or habit from when
task was task—not mine.

Task is placed, the ends dependent. I punch

in whether or not
the tools will befit
my tasks or grasp.

You form, watch our tools may yet out-spin us.

GUESS

I

The jacaranda, for instance, is beautiful
but not serious.

That much
I can guess.

And that the view
is softened by curtains.

That the present moment
is an exception,

is the queen bee
a hive serves,

or else an orphan.

2

So the jacaranda
is foreign and extravagant.

It gestures in the distance.

Between there and here
you ask

what game
we should play next week.

So we'll be alive
next week,

continuing
what you may or may not

mean to be
an impossible flirtation.

HEAVEN

1

It's a book
full of ghost children,

safely dead,

where *dead* means
hidden,

or wanting
or not wanting

to be known.

2

Heaven is symmetric
with respect to rotation.

It's beautiful
when one thing changes

while another thing
remains the same.

3

Fading redundancies.

Feathery runs.

Alternate wisps.

Imaginary
sprung striations.

Imaginary meaning
"seen by humans."

THE QUESTION OF FIRE

Because it pours color in its path.
Because all things in it come down to the bones of bones, some
    particles
more fundamental than dirt.
Because its roar reminds us of nothing.
Imagine a basket of flame: always emptying, always full.
Because it was begun from one word (tree) held too close
to another (lightning).
Because of embers, those handfuls of history, and the potential of
    matches—
a future that any careless carrying might ignite.
Because there is no net, no cure, no promise.
Because we have been captured.

Rapture: the first curl of smoke quickening into blue and how it
    grows up
the way a kiss surprises (only lips on lips yet
the body suffused with ticking)
so that suddenly it's a real engine-red.

The fingers of grass along the alley know it
but lean in anyway and are consumed.
Because it calls to be fed and feeding will never surfeit.
Because to live is to hunger and nothing is more alien
and more familiar than the hunger of another.

BONE MARROW HARVEST

Waiting for surgery, I see
the large sheeted backs
bent over the table
like the draped shoulders of the onlookers,
meant to be us, in the frescoes by Giotto
of the scenes of the miracles in Christ's life.
In *The Lamentation*, He reposes
in the arms of Mary, while Mary Magdalene
delicately lifts His feet,
regarding the holes from the nails,
like the way we were taught
to extend our hands in dancing school.
He is composed, being already dead,
but Mary, his mother, looks at him
searchingly as if she knows
they have not finished
their conversation.

Using a small hammer, the doctors drove
a sharp narrow tube into my hip
to extract the marrow. In the recovery room,
a small crescent moon cut
has appeared on my face.
My iliac crest is a livid, purple field.
The bruise runs down my buttocks
into my rear like a river seeking the delta.
Here and there are the black puncture wounds
pursed with plastic strips
that glint as I turn in the mirror, like mica.
This is my chance to be born again,
to go as close to death as they dare take me.

In the fresco
only the angels are agitated.
They tumble and cavort in the night sky
like children on the edge of a party.
The night behind them is a scrim.
Already the light of the resurrection fills the sky.

CHEST X-RAY

The pic line was threaded
up a vein in my arm, like an elastic
through a pants waist

In the x-ray room
against the light box
it showed up a pale white
shepherd's crook above
my heart. I saw the looming cliffs
where my death may begin;
the gate of my ribs;
and the two metal valves
that replaced my nipples
when they cut the cancer away.
The clavicles above
were like the bonnet tops of gates
to heaven or a cemetery

I saw the dark, unspecified shapes
of organs, blurred like a fish in a tank.
I saw the column of spools
that is my spin—the keel of the boat—
the long bones of my arms,
oars pulled in to rest,
the ark of my ribs
the vessel I will climb into
to bear me out of life.

FROM MY WINDOW

Columns of light slant away
from the bridge in the water
as if there were a room down there
and heaven were not above, but below.
From backyards come the voices of children
and as if my own mother were chanting
me back to childhood, the faint voice
of a woman crying a name again and again.
Church bells—four, five, six times—
fade up there among the pigeons. Those
I have loved left blurred footprints
in the snow, going off in directions
I could not understand. I try to think
of them here—breaths off the river.

How the lamps in the dusk
shine with a richer yellow part way out
onto the terrace below—but just beyond
the dark, the trees and all the faces
are waiting. Now, up here in this air
too pure yet to hold the darkness,
I want to live like the woodsman
led by lamps that lighted and dimmed themselves
as he passed, or like the child who dreams
she cannot step out from between
the tracks but does and lets the spell
of wandering overtake her, inventing a way
through the woods—until the moment when my mother
and father return as the one person
they will become in death. They bring
the elderbark cradle where I will curl
into the shape in which my mother has lain.

And I will rock all the way back
to childhood, the moments of my life
clear as though on the other side of glass, as they pass,
giving back to existence a substance
that leaves me like steam. Then those
I have loved who have died before me
will step forward, and standing
around the crib, godmothers and godfathers,
say to one another—"That's not she,
no she is somewhere else."

ON THE OBSERVATION DECK OF THE EMPIRE STATE BUILDING

This is the autumnal equinox,
but already night is rising, darkening
the thick smog like an ingredient
stirred from below. From the edge
I peer down at the city lights
the way sometimes I can see
all the way back to my childhood
down those streets at the end of the day
curiously quiet, except for a ball
bouncing again and again.
And I feel as when a child of three or four
I balanced at the top of the cellar stairs
until I felt a tug I didn't understand
and then pulled myself back.
And now I feel the feeling
I knew on spring afternoons
when I stood at my upstairs window
and let the air blow over me
and felt set apart from my self by life itself
and by another knowledge
acrid, like the smell of the metal screen
against my face. Later, I climbed the fire towers
and tops of tall buildings, clinging
to the handrails, watching
the ground leave me through gaps
between the steps, until
the land fell away into hills I had never seen
like a cloth shaken out and smoothed.

On the Eiffel Tower last summer
when failures in love felt like finding
again and again the one rotting step,
I climbed up and down, seeking
that shaky vertigo, the odd perspectives
a turn of events can give—
the sight of my life whole and yet oblique
like the buildings of Les Invalides;
seeking a sense of separateness,
of animal finiteness and fear:
one set of days lived,
the other whole and unformed
before me, like a point of equilibrium
where I could balance.
And I almost willed it to happen
as if I could plunge right then,
like the crazy boy, holding my treasure—
everything I had left.
Back inside the people give off warmth
by their numerous presence
and I let myself be comforted by their voices
unfocused and indistinct
the way I never could if I were listening.
Through the glass, the sky seems even more pale
and full of light, like the ceiling
of a room still lit after the guests have left.

SUMAC

Just outside my window, sumac berries
cluster, smaller than cherries—
shiny and firm and glistening.
All around me, fruit I may not eat—
my son who pushed from me
red and glistening, whom I savor
only in moments as if peering
through his kaleidoscope
which he brandishes like a baton,
or as if gazing into the mirror
of consciousness to see what is.
If I could husband my separateness
I would foster growth
like the eighty-four-year-old neighbor
retired to one acre, who tends
his garden so often
he has no predators;
he is his own scarecrow.
I glimpse him on nights
when the light seems to flow
from creation itself, stooping
over his garden as I used to bend
over my son's crib in the dark
to see his small archaic smile,
the smile of those who know
the love of God from within.
The neighbor tells me

he often doesn't sleep nights, just rests,
lying quietly, I think
in the valley of the shadow, along his furrows.
Now he is hovering among the stalks
with their long, dark, hidden husks
half unfurled; the lettuce
leaves pleated and frilled;
the small bulbs of melons just forming
under leaves; the cucumbers and peppers
dark and gleaming; the stumps
of broccoli lopped at the ground.

2 A.M.

This is the hour most likely to be your last
and so each morning I am awakened
for the blood pressure cuff
which inflates around my arm
like the puffed sleeve of a girlhood
dress; for two fingers lightly resting
on my pulse where the wrist corsage
was tied by Paul Thompson
when he took me to the senior prom.
Its scent reached me all night
from where my arm rested on his shoulder
during the slow dances in the darkened cafeteria.
So strange to be dancing with a body
pressed up against your own,
to smell hair oil and soap
exhaled breath
more important than a name
stepping backwards through the waltz
for the stethoscope
which reaches discreetly
into my hospital gown
like the hand of a boy
reaching for my breast.

IN THE RED DRESS I WEAR TO YOUR FUNERAL #8

I do not desist in my delusion do not permit the victor's history
will not admit your fake religion what jams your fingers
in the dry vagina of tin idylls will not will not go quietly

your evil goody who cries me in the marketplace who knocks
my ear to the pillory with false instruments my crimes never
crimes for firstly I be the pretty pony of all plague slant-gashed
a coil beneath my scum of loveliness No! I was I always am

your yellow roses in a beer bottle your weakness and reward
one organ conjoined in the blue tipi of floating whistles
doubled thunder coming in my wicked mouth to eat you and your
grandma too Name her! Name her who bites you harder little girl!
Will not say for seconds I am filth dirty as the damaged apple I bore
not yours never yours that unspeakable sunshine Turn your head!

Turn your head and I'll kindly cut it off! Yes Yes the best reason I am
left only the mother of a great sun you would go blind and blinder to
    look
upon its number and for finally I am not of your being being Queen
of the flat kingdom what crops your emptiness I do not admit these
    nor
I lied nor I betrayed nor I am starving for you nor can you make me
    never will I disappear

BLURRY EVIDENCE

The travel brochure should
be more sordid

so I looked at the steal of spring
where beading had gone slack,

sugar was on its knees,

lazy went the night cover.

Here's to you, blue morpho,
tagging the way with flirty soot.

Your glow remembers me
with a silver eye. Maybe you'll
give me a lift

and we'll find refuge

in a windy kitchen, take

a pan in hand, show our fancy
hats in the ruin, our envy coats

wrapped to a curtsy. Tragic

it may seem to a mirror, floored
and without manners,

and we wedge our way in,

but the game's unmerciful,
listen, listen.

CASCADE

What crouches outside my hut
                    tonight?
                                        Is it he with apologies?
        Or is it another he?   I have enough nuts
and dried fish to stay in here for days.

                        Stars now, just clicks
in the sky.   I let them circle my head, my loose tiara.

        What else can I shop for?   I'm kneeling and
something/someone journeys through

                        the damp corridors, stops at a figure
on the slippery walls.   An upside-down message

                                curls and uncurls. Someone

feels certain he can come here.
                        I know when to leave, when the sky

is ready. —Peel back, let me through.

PUMPKIN PICKING

The day we take our son into the orange fields to go pumpkin
    picking,
he proudly wheels the wagon through the muddied rows

stopping now and then to observe the pumpkins,
how one is lopsided, another the shape of a woman's torso,

one the size of an October moon. Before us the gray, fractured sky
so close you feel you could walk into it and enter the other world,

the air the kind of cold you pray for by August.
By the side of the road a man is burning leaves,

the smell drifts through the tangled rows, seeps into our wool jackets,
    our hair,
the way loss penetrates every aspect of a landscape, from a frozen

patch of ground, to this stand of blue spruce in the distance.
While my son is strutting down one row, up another, filling his wagon
    with pumpkins,

occasionally kicking one that has broken loose and begun to mold,
I've wandered further into the field through so many rows of orange
    heads

it's as if the souls of our lost children have entered this graveyard
where in a month's time the fields will be picked over, pumpkins
    splayed

open, smashed, left to rot. Ready to be pulped, seeds cleaned,
toasted, later carved into jack-o-lanterns for our table, these
   pumpkins haunt me.

How they grow wild, almost arbitrary, how they give so much
   meaning
to a boy I cherish. Look, their thick, husky umbilical stems that wed
   them to the ground,

how with a quick slice of a blade, even a hearty pull,
they are cast free from the earth toward heaven.

MARK BIBBINS

ENDING IN AN
ABANDONED MONTH

Of the citizenry but not exemplary,
another false copy of me returns
to cheap structures that poke
            into the clouds.

        Nauseous, we watch
a two-foot tornado stagger black
up our street, hear the sick smash
of windows hit by giant hailstones.

Every time the world
                ends this way,
I want to thank whoever had
a choice. Perhaps we should have

seen it coming—white kids giving
mad props to zombies, Jersey studs
with waxed eyebrows and brilliant
   buffed nails.   Should I specify

        that here I am with you,
the air a shade somewhere left
of flesh and right of slate, smeared
over our Manhattan as the snow

comes to blunt everything tonight?
Certainly there are too many
    species of weather,
        which is why they're

being replaced by color-coded models
of pure dread. When it's finally over,
years from now, when the storm ends,
            let whoever digs us

out find this headline—SHOOTING VICTIM
        APOLOGIZES TO VICE PRESIDENT—
so they can get a sense of how
    we did it when we died.

PHENOMENOLOGY
OF THE PRICK

You say, Let's get naked. It's 1962; the world
is changing, or has changed, or is about to change;
we want to get naked. Seven or eight old friends

want to see certain bodies that for years we've
guessed at, imagined. For me, not
certain bodies: one. Yours. You know that.

We get naked. The room
is dark; shadows against the windows'
light night sky; then you approach your wife. You light

a cigarette, allowing me to see what is forbidden to see.
You make sure I see it hard.
You make sure I see it hard

only once. *A year earlier, through the high partition between cafeteria*
booths, invisible I hear you say you can get Frank's
car keys tonight. Frank, you laugh, will do anything I want.

You seemed satisfied. This night, as they say,
completed something. After five years of my
obsession with you, without seeming to will it you

managed to let me see it hard. Were you
giving me a gift. Did you want fixed in my brain
what I will not ever possess. Were you giving me

a gift that cannot be possessed. You make sure
I see how hard
your wife makes it. You light a cigarette.

NO. 4

Suddenly I catch sight of a peculiar bulge in the grass beneath me.
I don't recall it's been around before.

I narrow my eyes and stretch my neck, then realize that
this is a dead man and his face buried in the soil.

— — —

She had tried to grab him before the fall,
but he slid away like an eel.

Then she knew no more.

The hand was transparent and etched in the mind
like an invisible fish hidden beneath a stone
at the bottom of the sea.

— — —

The noise suddenly increases, gets louder and percussive;
gathered in the end, it's the crack of a hammer
that echoes over and again until the thread is cut.

Then the silence, more than ever before.

And now I know how the last leaf must feel.

DIAGNOSIS

The doctor says think of it this way. Your insides are like the jungle at night: warm, noisy, rank with mango, and but for some holes drilled through the sky by stars, wholly dark. A river floats through you on its back, shivering with silver piranha. Banyan roots claw its face with thirsty fingers and draw black water up to the leafy canopy, where the last honeysuckle vireo on earth has sunk her beak into the single living pygmy anaconda, which in turn has the bird half wrapped in its flexing grip. Only one will live. It's too soon to say.

DEAD MAN'S WALLET

When waiting for anything or to fill in
the silent spaces standing in any kind of line,
I'll open my wallet and pretend it's a dead man's
because I'm always trying to make the familiar

strange. I stumbled across him reeking in the jungle
this morning; I hid the body safely, buried beneath the palms.
This time I didn't mind the money I suspected wasn't there,
satisfied enough with knowing this man's name and what photos

he carried (all easily explained), and I already surrounded
his ticket stub from 1994 with a story about love ending
sadly. The picture of Bela Lugosi, I'll admit, still troubles me
with possibility, but I think it connotes a man of complexity,

an artist type, a detective of himself who was, at one point,
upset that *The Paris Review* never responded, that no one
ever photographed him in black and white while he was brooding
or writing in his study with smoke (there simply *must* be smoke)

curling about his head like so many un-tethered, ghostly
thoughts. Such a photo, surely, would have been in his wallet
had it existed. It has been four or five hours since I buried the body,
and I don't feel suspicious or in any way wrong, but happy

in knowing that I would certainly be more missed than this man
had I disappeared in the jungle. The man holding *my* wallet
would hear sirens; have to face my face on posters and television.
Soon enough, I'd like to think, he'd have to answer tough questions.

LYNN CHANDHOK

PHUL CHUNAN

i.m. Anisha Dang, 1972—2003

At the cremation grounds, your father holds
my hand and says, *On my verandah, late
at night, I'd hear the wind chimes that she hung
and think, 'My daughter is so beautiful.'*

Behind him, priests are washing off your bones
so loudly that I barely hear the rest—
I never climbed the stairs to tell her so.

When someone hands me marigolds, I take
my turn and drop them in the bright bronze urn.
The lid is closed. The ribbon seems too red.

At Gangotri, where they'll finally let you go,
the marigolds will mark your progress, bright
like grace notes on the currents, like the words
I wish I'd heard, and wish I could have spoken.

SEVEN INFIDELITIES

One kind of night you walk into,
fog unstitches everything, bodiless
streetlamps, pencil-sketched men appear
and disappear. The sound of whipping
but nothing is touching. A man lies
down on the pavement and the imprint
he leaves looks nothing like him.

— — —

After ten years. He must have known
her body, that she shaved up to
the thigh only. He spent five hours
at the gym each day, recruiting
his neck muscles, lifting riverbeds in sets,
as they flowed past her house, like muddy
veins. Where she stood every day to see
if he drove by.

— — —

A phone message that the new girl had
burned my favorite blue sweater. Imagine
the sweater, with its wristless arms,
illuminating her face. Later, the man
on top of her gave her a blue sweater.
And I woke in a new city with cable cars
glued to metal tracks, sparks from buses
like flashbulbs, a layer of fog, light
as breath on my body.

— — —

A woman on a self-guided tour squints
behind a velvet rope, at the family portrait,
Going to the Opera. I recognize her look—
the desire to be in that living room, under
the crease of light, closed in that dress
with a train. Soon to be tongued by
a Vanderbilt dressed in black.

— — —

A professor's wife passed her husband's
lover, stood against the pewter
of the ocean, smelled the saline of
her country, dove down into
the blank sheet, crested a wave
with her fin, glided like paper under
whaling boats, back to ether, to oil, to
carbon atoms, to half of nothing, nothing.

— — —

A tall Asian man lives three doors down.
Married to a short Caucasian nurse.
No snow to mask the lamppost, flagless
mailboxes, tree held up by two wooden stakes.
I want a better story. Wood smoke, then,
red leaves brought down early by the storm.
A tall handsome Asian man. Good hair,
good shoes. Lifts open the shutters
every time I jog past in the snow.

— — —

I want to make out with Professor X tonight,
the girl says. But she's late to the last
barn dance of the last night of the conference.
The wood floors begin to shake as an
animal cage might. Somewhere in Asia,
houses fall into an ocean with all the people
bumping into sofas. Outside the barn,
the snow falls in the shape of men and women,
and they collide randomly in the dark.

RECUMBENT

"I have never been on a coach that was going fast enough for me."

—EMERSON

And I have never been on a couch
that was going fast enough for me,
not even in the indolence of youth
or the lassitude of these winter afternoons.

I have known a few zippy ones,
a green davenport that seemed designed
for high-speed wool-gathering
and a sofa upholstered in a pattern

of needlepoint leafage and rabbits
that could carry me rapidly from one place to another.
I remember traveling from a teacup
to one of the rings of hell and back

one summer morning in a small apartment
in a large chaotic city,
and another time, going from a picture
of a wolf enclosed in a wooden frame

to a real wolf standing in the snow
in what seemed like a matter of seconds.
But more often, I go nowhere but to sleep.
Where is the steering wheel on this thing?

I think as I sink deeper in the cushions,
the last of the twilight fading away,
the white cat kneading my stomach
with paws so pink and fortified with claws.

Translated by Eliot Weinberger and Iona Man-Cheong

CALL

Early morning invented by shivering birds
the peach tree comes to juicy conclusions
women praised by the hills
sew up the sea with rays of light

a bell-sound takes off across the morning
reaches the tops of our heads
and we turn around
deniers of the times
scorpion breeders of memory
and the street musician on the corner
playing to the vast melancholic wind

where the question turns around
to become an answer
in this forbidden year
a crow stands on one leg:
his writing experience

why do books make such a racket?
the anger of their conclusions

Translated by Eliot Weinberger and Iona Man-Cheong

THE OLD CASTLE

Those roses a cause of shame
like the truth of this clan
letting you linger for a long while

the fountain traces back the first thread of light
in the darkness of reproduction
stagnant water swallows
the arrogant flame on the carved relief

the pine hedge labyrinth is a grammar
find the way out and you can speak
follow the flight of stairs
deep into this language
unobstructed corridors and hidden passages
lead to that echoing hall

you shout out loud, there is no echo

portraits surround you
the last generation of hostesses
slip off their old-age masks

drinking water from desire's cup
her eyes carry a cat
beyond the boundaries of life
zero degrees, sound of a piano rippling
someone else's calendar
a tomorrow that never returns

1916: the arrowheads of war
point in all directions
she spreads the white tablecloth
to invoke the art of starvation
as the light of the last candle
reports the century's storm
she dies of starvation

a well, the earth's single eye

you touch the candlestick
that frozen hand
gripping the flame
the pigeons she raised
make their nests in the clan silence

hearing the sighs of tomorrow
the main gate clangs shut
art is dead
roses bloom

FRANCESCA CAN TOO STOP THINKING ABOUT SEX, REFLECT UPON HER POSITION IN POETRY, WRITE A REAL SONNET.

pilgrim, i did not mean to be so loose
of tongue, so bold in all i loosely told
in my smut so smug, so overly sold.
i did not mean, pilgrim, to traduce.

i apologize, i offer no excuse:
but, poet, though you have right to scold
it was high-souled you who made my mouth hold
what it held and tell what it told. a truce,

no, let's call it an honor. mine is apt,
as far as long sentences go: my vice
in your verse will tempt others to try

and sing: readers, lovers forever rapt
and about to sweetly sigh: paradise!
thank you, poet, for keeping me alive

FRANCESCA SAYS MORE

that maiden thump was book on floor, but
does it really matter who kissed who
first or then who decided to go further?
lower? faster? naturally we took
turns on top. *now here, now there, and up*
and down . . . once it started no one even thought to think to stop.
so, we have holes inside our souls,
but mustn't we begin by filling others'?
god gave us lips and hands and parts
that cannot possibly be saved for prayer, nor by,
i will not name names, but turns out not
the only cunning linguist i, who chants my lay.
it's you, white pilgrim, whom next galehot seeks.

fuck. we didn't read again for weeks.

(AND MORE)

(o (l)uxu/orious (p)/(l)ussuria) one can rule
rimini and still not rule (or rim) me. doric, ionic,
phallic: i liked it all. i moaned and wept as i do now,
but it was a joy and a different kind of sorrow:
to see your lover's eyes when he's down there. down there
the very root *was* the very root, and fig was fruit and nut
gelato. down here how it happened can still make me shudder:
sigh
just how far down, sinner, must you go? whatever pleases you:
follow my tail, my thigh. and: VIDE FICA MIA. eat my furbelowed
heart, tremble at my furbo and my body gone but still beautiful
heart, this life that's for the birds is saved by the rhyming such as our
heart, if you twist my arm just right i'll lose my mind.

the new style is the old style: from behind.

OLENA KALYTIAK DAVIS

FRANCESCA SAYS TOO MUCH

each day i came an infinity of times; it rained reign
was so complete with every pleasure as if in love i sang.
pity you're confused: 'twasn't love. it was sex that dissolved me:
limo was body and mud. and long and shiny
and briny what i polished with my tongue marmo hard and pallina
smooth once whetted i never stopped saying sipa, was always in
position, in the mood, too much was never enough. i kept open
my arms my legs my eyes my lips moving lifted to heaven
my ass my hips. pilgrim, can you picture it? my tits. and it was
all we. don't cry. dry your ablutionary tears. no thing now can absolve
    me:
but i regret it not: i was so alive! o, to again have
someone's occhi and fingers and penes on in me, to be
licked and sucked and eaten and fucked and debauched.

sigh and sign and eye hungry pilgrim, if only you could have watched.

YOU ART A SCHOLAR, HORATIO, SPEAK TO IT

You say you walk and sew alone?
I walk and sew alone.

You say you gape and waver?
I am mostly dizzy, most open-mouthed.

You say you taste it with each dish?
I drink it and I spit it up.

You say it lays you facedown?
I kiss the dirt.

Carved into your bone china?
Mine's more fine.

Folded into your laundry?
Dry. Dry. Dry.

Is it quite awful and unbearable?
Quite.

Is it sweet and gentle?
Most sweet, most gentle.

Does it make you retch?
I am wretched.

Do you write it poems?
I compose on it daily.

Is it epic?
In thought and in treatment.

Do you cry upon it?
It is flat and wet.

Will you humor it?
Forever.

Will you forsake it?
Never.

You say you keep it in a box?
I've Cornelled mine.

You say you call it soft names?
I call it softly. I name it.

Clipped of fledge?
Clipped of fledge.

You say it sits up on your soul?
It has it licked.

A new religion?
Nay, a faith.

Do you take it to bed?
I've pillowed and I've laid with it.

Does it propagate?
I sharpen my chastity upon it.

I belt it. I go down on it.
I keep it down.

Have you done your best to bury it?
I have dug.

With half a heart?
With dull spade, yea, half-heartedly.

Has it a sword?
A long-tailed lion on its crest.

Would you unknow it?
I've called it bastard.

Bastard!
Would you divorce it?

Untie it, would you?
Have you

Done with it?
No. I will have more.

ALEŠ DEBELJAK

Translated by Christopher Merrill

HOMECOMING

A crust of thin ice cracks and signposts change. Summer snow
slides down the Karavanke mountains. Pale princely faces. Blood
will soon return to their cheeks. The frozen woodpecker's knock
against the windowpanes awakens us. Early morning. Light teems

from cracks in the earth. What a melancholy odor rises from the
    boots
exhausted by the deep marsh! Above the roofs, winds from the west
    and south
mix, and blindness ends on the threshold of the grave. Now all of us
    who
left home at birth gather at this holy hour. No one needs the broken

eggshell. From its pieces emerges the map of a country which defies
oblivion. In the square, the tank trap is again at a standstill. An old
    woman
lovingly raises her arms free of desire and fear. The mystery of ten
    days

is over. She awaits them peacefully, recognizing the despair under
    their helmets.
They think she is their mother comforting them. The face of a
    soldier
old as a Celtic vase drowns in the murmuring water that might fill
    the dry well.

ALEŠ DEBELJAK

Translated by Christopher Merrill

WOMAN'S SHADOW

What you implanted in my marrow I translate into a language
I haven't mastered yet: the cadence of a scream reaching
into the heart, the rumbling of an underground train, church
naves without altars, gods murmuring in the pelvis. You:

you rose from a shell like a delicate sculpture from the furnace
of a glass-blower. You taught me anguish and humility
before the gospel of a demanding prophet. And the freedom
of a doe bounding across the meadows of a slumbering heaven.

I can't reach them without you. I hear the chestnuts crackling
on the terraces of my village. The asphalt is cooling. I don't care.
I'd rather tremble with delight, like a house on the verge of
    restoration,

when you sing a new melody. At the darkest hour of the day you show
    me
the alphabet of wind and fate and seeds. I read stains in history's
    cellar.
I know my home will be there, where you mark off the wild garden.

$6.82

My economy is circular: I earn money from an institution that owns
   most of the businesses where I tend to spend most of my money.

My economy is quasi-medieval, trade-centered, and guild-like.

My economy is not arch-canonical.

My economy is a misfortune that recently befell me.

My economy admits foundational narratives.

My economy is language.

My economy is the executioner's reversal of fortune.

My economy has no essential features.

My economy admits parallax critiques of ideology.

My economy owes something to over three thousand dead soldiers.

My economy does not intimate and would rather not split hairs about
   what belongs to whom.

My economy can't stay out of things, but can't make it into the thick
   of things either.

My economy has questionable purchasing power.

My economy has no surrogate.

My economy has no interpretive skills but is rife with interpretive communities.

My economy is of trees chopped down in Brooklyn, and the gradual encircling of brick.

My economy is the new red.

My economy thrives on shades of gray.

My economy is an unremarkable tuna sandwich that is missing the slices of tomato I had asked for.

My economy is a liter bottle of Poland Spring water coming not from Poland but from Maine and bought at a university cafeteria in Uptown Manhattan where there are quite a number of water fountains that deliver water with a funky metallic aftertaste.

My economy is a poem called "First Purchase of the Month," consisting of two stanzas with six eight-word lines each within a larger poem that could be endless but won't be:

> Could've been an outfit for the Whitney Biennial
> Couldn't afford one, nor did I need it.
> Who cares how you look at the zoo;
> it's about the animals, stupid. Which reminds me,
> could've been the trail mix I snacked on
> & which I managed *not* to purchase myself.

> It was tuna on whole wheat, lettuce, jalapeños;
> a one-liter bottle of water (Poland Spring).
> Asked for tomato too, which the lady forgot.
> You Puerto Rican, she asked? Don't think so,

said another one in Spanish. Let me answer.
No, what made you think so? The peppers?

My economy needs contractions and abbreviations.

CITY OF GODS

Thistly Augustine, disser of the shy world, I cannot consider your
    city.
I cluck my tongue at the sun & sky. The sky rises
too steeply. My soul can go
no higher than the highest highway billboard.

Oh Pericoli on a boat, a Mongoose, a motorcycle—you can't
draw the gods of New York from New Jersey.
Just across the cosseted alley they sit: the gods in the dark, eating
    fishsticks.

The best god I ever saw is my mother named Betsy.

Then-a-days, in the blackout of '77, from my roof I could feel
the gods sweating and moving. Some got trapped in elevators,
some got into black clothes & looted the glass-front stores.

No one was whispering Icarus! Phaethon! Glory glory golden!
I waited—to open my eyes and see my shy mother leaning over me.

I could feel dark stacked mortar, higher than the sun. I was great &
    complete
in that stack. The dark. The worldly world. The doth corrupt of
    Augustine
doth. I am corrupted by the beautiful sweating & moving.

Did you hear the divine shuffling across soft tar, the gods going
toward the girls sleeping out on the roof? The gods felt like
soft sootfall in my ears then. The world is never too much with us,
said the ash. Go back down into the dark rooms, said the ash,
ask Giovanna if her mother still loves me.

I was a girl and a fleck of rust then. I was a girl and a poorly lit room.
On the roof, I was a clothesline thief trying on camisoles,
graying camisoles hung out to dry between the antennae,
and a god in a window across the way would watch me.

Hey god in the window, god of loneliness, god of smelly spaces
stacked with newspapers, god of walks home from the L before the
    light ends,
if I ask you to please turn my sooty camisole into wings
and me into an industrial moth, I am asking to be man-made—
I don't want to be this girl anymore.

FROM NOWHERE WITH LOVE

at the end of December, My Sweetheart,
   My Delectable Darling. Maybe next time
      we meet there will be less tension. Maybe
         next time you'll enter stage-left as Nina,
            our femme fatale, all angles, a cigarette

in one white-gloved hand, and still gloriously
    misunderstood by my better self, a thin plume
       of smoke rising from a puddle of bubbling wax.
          What's left after all my neuroses have been put out?
             See, I've begun to count, dearest, and really, there's no

end to it. All of our enths are used up,
   all our Marchembers, all those mango-
      butter back rubs late nights in your dusty
         basement apartment. Once, you told me
           everything I never wanted to know about

heart attacks, followed by an exhausting history
    of the Balkans. I wanted to scream, strike a fist against
       my breast, for how might I sleep again with your warm body
          next to mine? O wicker armchair, O Nina Simone, O ladies
             and gentlemen of the jury: we never made love, hardly
              kissed,

but talked and talked until the tension waned,
    until wine and weakness made it almost easy to lie
       down in one bed together. Almost. And now, now
         you live in a city named after the howls I make nightly
           into my pillow. Now your new cat has chewed through

our lines of communication. Now you're with a man
  who does not dance, but who plays the violin and eats
    well. Do send me a message every so often, Pookie.
      Tell me you remember that boy who painted his shoes
        one night so they'd be two-toned for the masquerade,

how immediately they began to crack
  and flake. Tell me you haven't forgotten
    the girl who wrote that life better always feel
      like too goddamned much, the girl who sat staring

at her antiseptic blinds in the near morning,
  listening for the creak that meant I'd shut the gate,
    gone home, and now she could figure out just which
      song she and her smoke-filled room might play next.

MATTHEW DICKMAN

APOLOGY AND WINTER THINGS

In the book of Mark a home is built like a beehive, inside
it's a shining comb. A place to face each other in the light.
This is not my home. My home, constantly turning, has four walls
filled up with winter things: a north wind and pine cones, a cord
of wet wood. In the yard the leaves rot. The stone basement fills
up with sticks our dog spits out, the soft bodies of mice our cat
has worked into a pulp of fur and mud: Christmas
has never come so slowly. In the dark I wait for it to appear
like parents in a doorway, like my dark siblings appearing
from their wax cells: in the bathroom my sister removes her
bandages, in the bedroom my brother hides himself under a bunk,
chews his sucking-thumb. In the kitchen my mother holds me up
by my wrists and shakes me until I am sorry. I *am* sorry. She loves me.
In the book of Mark the mother and son are different: they hardly
   touch.

SOME OF THE MEN

I had to walk around for a long time before I could see anything

The leaves
circling down the street
imitating the insides of seashells
imitating
my fingerprints

I could sense my father
sitting alone in his little white Le Car
staring off at the empty parking lot

No radio
No wind
No birds

Just some guy in his car looking out at the blacktop and the shadows
    of telephone wires

It isn't a sad scene, not really

Some of us are getting
exactly what we asked for

Some of us
don't even have
to wait

———

Think of my grandfather, still drunk or asleep, passed out on top of
    my grandmother

so she has to wait for him
to come to

along with the late
Redwood City morning
the light skipping in
across

the swimming pool

The smell of failed sex
bourbon and
chlorine

Dead cigars

He taught me how to swim

with one of his hands beneath my legs and another beneath my
    stomach
how to cup my hands, how
to turn my head

Inhale and exhale
and move gracefully
through liquid

— — —

Look at
Josh's father—

Stumbling into the bedroom at three in the morning the two of us
    asleep and all that moonlight
    and beat his son's
    head against

the headboard

You fucker you fucker you asked for it

The moon

His jaw splashed across the pillowcase

— — —

The Parietal   Temporal   Occipital
The Atlas and Axis
Spheroid and
Spheroid

The real smile
real grin

Your movable and immovable joints

Your eyes
your orbits

Sutures

If given the chance
I would

break them all

— — —

For a long time my grandfather
tried to kill anyone
who came near him

Wives
Daughters
Stepdaughters

What is it called when insects are stuck forever in a kind of amber?

Then he got sick
and he was going to die anyway
and he stopped
trying to kill people

Then we could fall in love

———

My father's advice is claustrophobic and flat as it fills the soft leather
    booth inside the restaurant

Birthday lunch
Red neon
Cigarettes

What you need to do
is join the Army, the Marines
something

You need to be taught a lesson

———

Some of the men are standing in their backyards at night, looking up
    at the stars
        listening to the freeway

Their hands in their pockets

Everything's just
as it was

My hands
in my pockets, curled
into tiny
fists

My belt buckle

gleaming

BERET SPOTTING

The other other afternoon after
a hearty brunch of nectarine squab,
scrambled egg whites & wet toast,
coffee juice grapefruit juice & port,
a fine cake made mostly of air & sweet spindles,
followed by a nap on the prototypical orange
square did I realize there was still time.

Cough drops, trillennia. Umm, spirals:
there was still time for beret spotting:

so I hoofed down the bony boulevard
toward the hectic, peach-pit esplanade.

My prior imbibing cost me my good breath.
—Nothing kills me how the hiccups kill,
trust, if manufactured and implemented
as torture, had I a state, or a secret,
I would blurt them quick as the mention—this
from one who would happily test the
Punishing Shoes or the Heretic's Fork for

just a second. Or even the Head Crusher,
minus the skull-steadying spike. Maybe even the Iron Maiden

or the Judas Cradle. Perchance the Hard Rock. Forget about
the Rack, the Pear, the Boots, the Saw, and the Wheel.

I'll have none of the monosyllabic devices.
"Launois *et al.* collected the words for hiccup
in 23 languages. Many, but not all of them,
are onomatopoeic. In English at least,

the sound of a hiccup and the burp it produces
are considered embarrassing but there is no help for it."

Since there is no help, come let us piss & fart;

"A hiccup is essentially an abrupt Mueller maneuver.
The glottis closes to prevent inspiration

35 milliseconds after electrical activity rises above the
baseline in the diaphragm and external intercostal muscles."

Were it not for my glottis closing, I may never
have spasmd upon the trail of crayons.
For I seldom watch the ground walking, but,
so convulsd, noted there were crayons there.
Poor child, to hoof alone that path
humping a 64-pack still fresh,
unstained by the complete page, unstained Flesh

(since '62 called peach)
unstained Melon, Maize, Green-Yellow,

unstained Salmon, Thistle, Yellow-Green,
unstained Raw Sienna, Hot Magenta,

unstained Black. White. Unstained Gray.
Poor child, the path to you melts
in radiant pools, in a sun the same
as yesteryear's. I thought. I thought
what you thought I'd think: "I must
find you. Whatever if the wax stains my shift,
whatever calico." You know, I began to follow

gathering wickless crepe-wrapped tallows.
The trail fell behind the arc that the world is.
Incidentally a very meager world one day only.
Forty-four colors to the azure, cerulean, very pretty sky.
Which, incidentally.

I followed, you were nowhere found to be.
Nay, I have done, you get no more of me.
But these flowers where which I got lazy
are there. I there, locked looking. Spammd
again. So delicate and damp the physiological individuality
despite the scores of scores in near facsimile
hooded reddening bulbs sweet spindles.
It just feels "naughty."

"How do they survive the big-time wind?"
"They don't have to, this is an asylum."

Which explains, I suppose, why I spot no berets.
Berets worn so the wind will take them spinning, spinning over the
    blubber moonishness!

Berets of various colors. Like hiccup. Berets,
which split from the soft bark of hollow fallen trees and spill their
    splendor somewhere.

SATELLITE CONVULSIONS

When I bend back to gaze at the satellite convulsions, I
am an aqueduct for twilit rain. Quite literally I stand

in the littoral zone: a lens—no, an aqueous humor, my
feet on the land below the high watermark, my hand

a glazed waver: *hello light-purple lights, hello red spots,*
you've beaten the stars out tonight but you're struggling with the

atmosphere aren't you? Over centuries the river became not
a river: Lethe's ends crept together—self-scavenging sea

snake—& the middle filled with water—morphology dubbed it
a lake & now the moon swims in it & the moon orbits it &

the moon tidally tugs on it. The moon is a satellite in a fit
of paroxysm. One minute past, I emptied an aluminum can

of dull opiate to the drains to wash down my antipsychotics
& then Lethe-wards slunk I. There must be this wire shaking

loose in my mind, an unattended firehose, a spasmodic
filament attempting to cool the baby planet but *lacerating*

precious gray matters. Thought leaves no vacancy for memory—
I forget & forget the rules, the thirst an auger; rain only whetting

it, I bend & lap some lake up, tongue it, suck the silty mammary
right where a light from the firmament meets it. I keep forgetting

the rules, a Ptolemaniac with stars & suns circling me; I keep
missing my cues, can't arrange the particles moments are made of—

and it's all good!—because when I bend seriously back & peep
at the satellite convulsions I am a sluiceway for night rain. If I love

at least I love aptly, terminally, like a man who loves his dinner until
he's done with it, then settles to the couch to easy pixilated dreams

(bounced off, yes, satellites, & beamed into a pale dish). And still,
even unfettered by history or hope, the world does not seem

shocking—simply something to fly a canvas balloon around, to
dig a hole in. To climb into. To allow to fill with water, perhaps

it is raining, perhaps you dig below the watertable; it gushes through
the dirt; your bath is drawn & in it are drawn (sputniks & stars) maps

& charts with which to constellate your body. Connect the dots.
A little ladle with four handles—a tiny light strobes in the cup, in hot

convulsions of distance, bleats of temporal ignorance, synapse of
    morse
but no code, blood but no pulse, the stream but no mouth or source.

THE WAR IS OVER

Not an acquiescence of surrender,
the bra hung from the flagpole.

The bra is black & there is no wind for once.
For once there is no wind & a spark that is a bird
brings a straw to an empty C-cup. A spark

that is a spark. That is the sun on the steel pole.
That is the oldest thing & then is gone, like the war,

whose trench is gone, because it is full of
red iron-clot soil, because there are lawnchairs
reclined on top of it (empty, but warm, still warm,

sweat-wet & stretched-out) & a white plastic table
with a pitcher of dark iced tea upon it.

The ice is half melted. Clear water waits near the brim.
The wasp waving in it annoys a piece of dust so minute
it might not be there. In its head is only enough space

for a split second of a song it heard the third of July, a trombone
     belch
muted with a pink plunger-head. The war was over again,
the parade began hitchless, history was history, a refugee

pinned a Purple Heart on a brave bomb & a drop of brown
blood rolled down its chest like a tumbling tumbleweed

as the saints came marching in in white fur hats, in white plastic
shoes, in tuxedoes matching the color-scheme of decrepit glory,
glockenspieled, anacondad in sousaphones, a trombone

with a wasp on its brass bell resting its wings.
It is pausing on my reflection, mid-tone, in the center of my stain.

Then there is snapshot of the sky departing generously,
perhaps forever. Appropriately dark, we finally see the "grand finale"
& realize it is only the preceeding parts pushed closely together

& we think we are all a bit relieved,
although we are afraid to admit even this.

TO THE ENGRAVER OF MY SKIN

I understand the pact is mortal,
agree to bear this permanence.

I contract with limitation; I say
no and no then yes to you, and sign

—here, on the dotted line—
for whatever comes, I do: our time,

our outline, the filling-in of our details
(it's density that hurts, always,

not the original scheme); I'm here
for revision, discoloration; here to fade

and last, ineradicable, blue. Write me!
This ink lasts longer than I do.

WATERMELON SODA

Key West

Pink scuttle
(a roasted pink,
like pork

in Chinese restaurants):
these claws poke out
from the pull-top

opening
of an empty can
of watermelon soda,

which clicks along
the sidewalk,
wobbling cylindrical

and alarming
beneath weary palms
accustomed to

the homeless.
Strange island,
to yield a walking

hot-pink soda can
inhabited by a lucky,
Modernist crab,

carrying on his back
a tropic shelter
by Barragan

or Le Corbusier,
perennially modish
if not quite practical,

since the candy-pink
pop can tips
and gyros

as he proceeds,
unstable island
—housed in style,

or hobbled by it?
The pink metal
flashes in the sun,

and seems worth it.
Or did yesterday.
This morning, after

the all-night storm,
where's he gone, our exile?
Floated clean away.

THE LONG QUEEN

The Long Queen couldn't die.
Young when she bowed her head
for the cold weight of the crown, she'd looked
at the second son of the earl, the foreign prince,
the heir to the duke, the lord, the baronet, the count,
then taken Time for a husband. Long live the Queen.

What was she queen of? Women, girls,
spinsters and hags, matrons, wet nurses,
witches, widows, wives, mothers of all these.
Her word of law was in their bones, in the graft
of their hands, in the wild kicks of their dancing.
No girl born who wasn't the Long Queen's always child.

Unseen, she ruled and reigned; some said
in a castle, some said in a tower in the dark heart
of a wood, some said out and about in rags, disguised,
sorting the bad from the good. She sent her explorers away
in their creaking ships and was queen of more, of all the dead
when they lived if they did so female. All hail to the Queen.

What were her laws? *Childhood*: whether a girl
awoke from the bad dream of the worst, or another
swooned into memory, bereaved, bereft, or a third one
wrote it all down like a charge-sheet, or the fourth never left,
scouring the markets and shops for her old books and toys—
no girl growing who wasn't the apple of the Long Queen's eye.

Blood: proof, in the Long Queen's color,
royal red, of intent; the pain when a girl
first bled to be insignificant, no cause for complaint,
and this to be monthly, linked to the moon, till middle age
when the law would change. *Tears*: salt pearls, bright jewels
for the Long Queen's fingers to weigh as she counted their sorrow.

Childbirth: most to lie on the birthing beds,
push till the room screamed scarlet and children
bawled and slithered into their arms, sore flowers;
some to be godmother, aunt, teacher, teller of tall tales,
but all who were there to swear that the pain was worth it.
No mother bore daughter not named to honor the Queen.

And her pleasures were stories, true or false,
that came in the evening, drifting up on the air
to the high window she watched from, confession
or gossip, scandal or anecdote, secrets, her ear tuned
to the light music of girls, the drums of women, the faint strings
of the old. Long Queen. All her possessions for the moment of time.

FOR MANY YEARS

Some nights I had to go there,
where I could not dare to stay.

No white dividing line made it clear
which side of the road was mine,

and when I parked and got out
no moon streaked a path.

I knew the way *by heart*.
That was the kind I had.

I'd give the equivalent of a sop
to Cerberus, and walk right in.

Ruin, with whom I'd come to flirt,
as usual was looking good.

I just needed to smell her perfume,
spend a little time under her spell.

Never was it easy getting back.
You can't trust a heart,

its attachments to the new,
how quickly it forgets its way.

The dog would awaken and bark.
And the story of how I got lost

in the navigable dark
each time needed to feel true.

GROOVALLEGIANCE

for Michael Veal

A dream. A democracy. A savage liberty.
And yet another anthem and yet another heaven
and yet another party wants you.
Wants you wants you wants you.
Wants you to funk-a-pen funkapuss.
Wants you to anthologize then retroop your group.
Wants you to recruit prune juice.
My peeps.
My poetics.
My feet.
All one.
All one.
All one, heel and toe.
My peeps.
My poetics.
My feet.
All one.
All one.
All one, lowly heel and toe.
Br'er feet and br'er beat repeatedly beaten.
Repeatedly beaten repeatedly beaten.
Br'er feet and br'er beat repeatedly beaten.
Repeatedly beaten repeatedly beaten repeatedly beaten.
Br'er feet and br'er beat repeatedly beaten.
Feet feet feet.
Every feet a foot and free, every feet a foot and free,
every feet a foot and free.
A foot and free.
Agony and defeat, a foot and free.
A foot and free.
Every feet a foot and free, every feet a foot and free,

every feet a foot and free.
    A foot and free.
    Agony and defeat, a foot and free.
    A foot and free.
    Reverend feet, a foot and free. Reverend feet,
repeatedly beaten.
    Feet feet feet.
    A million marchers.
    Two parties.
    One Washington.
    One Washington.
    Two parties.
    A million marchers.
    An afterparty.
    An afterparty after marching.
    The aftermarch.
    An aftermarch-afterparty after marching
all the way to Washington.
    Another march another party.
    Another afterrmarch after another afterparty.
    After another afterparty after marching.
    After another march afterpartying and after marching
all the way to Washington.
    Always Washington always Washington.
    Uncle Jam, enjambed
all the way to Washington.
    After all that marching after all that partying.
    Uncle Jam, enjambed.
    Always Washington.
    A million marchers.
    Two parties.

One Washington.
One Washington.
Two parties.
A million marchers.
Footwork.
If feet work for page shouldn't feet work
for stage, run-on.
Run-on platform.
Run-on floor,
run-on.
If feet work abroad shouldn't feet work
at home, run-on.
Run blood, run-off.
From run flag.
From run bag,
 run-on.
Run and tell it.
Run tell tag run tell toe, run tell, tell it.
De-decorate intelligence.
If so also de-decorate form. If so also de-decorate war,
run home.
In every war bloods leave and bloods bleed
and don't come home. What for in every war,
what for, and don't come home.
For war for war for war.
In every war bloods leave and bloods bleed
and don't come home. What for in every war,
what for, and don't come home.
For more for more for more.
That for, in every war.
That for, for every drug.
The war on drugs is a war on bloods,
run tell it.
A line is played. A section plays.
All up, into it, and involved, into it into it
and involved, all up into it and involved.
Footnote.

Take joke.
Take note to toes.
Clip note.
Go home.
Take note to foot.
Race note.
Footnote to feet.
Foot hurt.
Footnote to note.
Cite hurt.
Toe note to foot.
Bottoms up.
Sorefoot to church.
Stop running.
If office if oath.
Broken votes.
A line is played. A section plays.
A protest you press to test repeating itself.
A section plays. A line is played.
A protest you press to test repeating itself.
My peeps.
My poetics.
My feet.
Some ally.
Some enemy.
Mostly tradition.
The jive end.
Br'er rear.
Br'er rear end isms.
Pass out the words.
The kitty is not a toy.
    I owe roots and books to groundwork's underground crosstalk
of African Telephone Churches.
    All one all one all one, star-spangled funky.

MARCUS GARVEY VITAMINS

a

All us we *folk*
person community first.
Invent truth,

b

no he didn't,
yes he *did*. Ain't English.
You *lyin'* to me.

c

Africa dis*agrees*
with subject-verb agreement.
Aspect ratio,

d

widescreen whiteache.
Don't like it, *don't* Pulitzer me.
I stress less than land*less*ness.

e

I break beat, I rhetorical strategy,
I escape route.
I, I, I, *sike*.

THOMAS SAYERS ELLIS

WAYS TO BE BLACK IN A POEM

You'll need a talk, an oral walk,
Something natural and recognizable by your folk,
Something of music something of meaning,
A style capable of running-off at-the-mouth
When Massa AmEuroBrit Lit irks you most,
A little something-something of ancestry
And the courage not to accept any award

        that helps you
        and hurts others.

You'll need "Saturation,"
Your own profanity of Sundays,
Breakfast and Blackfist.
Wherever there is living You must listen
For the   *if* and *when*   the vernacular gives birth again.
You will need more than reference
Coulda   woulda   shoulda
And more than edjumacation.

You may even need to sell you and buy you,
      So low
           So long
                Sold
Or to slant yourself into a container whose symbolism
Is unknowingly superior
To standard usage,

A brilliant Attitude loved by Good.

CANCELED FLIGHT

I.

How many days,
     nights has it been
         without birds'

flighty upheavals,

coquettish bird-bathery,

flashing their blatant *V* ?

Birds that sing in Chinese and Sanskrit,
how slowly I walk without them.

2.

Into what other zone,

other story, other poem
have they flown?

In what other city
do they hatch
their bird-brained schemes?

The trees go on
as if nothing has changed.

3.

Remember how the moon
would flap its silver wings?

There were more stars too.

The sky was always busy
behind our backs
teeming with gods and angels.

Maybe birds never existed
or only in ancient times like Homer's.

I am trying to draw one from memory.

It has rosy cheeks,

     a galloping heart,

the rest—a vague softness.

     4.
Early in summer,
I dreamt they fell out of the sky
like the first drops of rain.

Planted themselves
     upside down in the earth,

strange flowers
brewing trouble,

wings, a pulpy fruit.

And now—not even a feather.

5.
ex-cardinals
ex-pigeons
ex-robins
ex-finches

ex-starlings
ex-sparrows

expatriate birds
that shit on sentiment
and refuse to ornament
our lawns

ex-nightingales
that pause mid-song
for a very, very long time

faster than thought
can cross a blank sky

FOUR PLANES OF EXPERIENCE

I. Reception & Contemplation

Whenever I walk the dog at dusk,
a certain silence of breath. Hitch-knot
over an ear. My split condition:

always cleaving, taking leave.
The branches' synaptic map, a wind
within the wind. Two sawhorses

say Fire & Rescue—how about
no fire, no retinue needed?
The maple that drops its green

rather than submit to a long
fall: preventative. At a certain age,
certain slow-growth cancers occur

in all patients. To consider this
stand of pines is to will a screech
owl who wakes at dusk to hunt

its limits, the word *pine* a home
calling in the shadow of its beak.
Who hasn't wished for greater returns

from Benefits Services agents?
Of course the hours proceed like this,
fingers along suspicious moles,

the splitting veins. Someone I know
calls her hours of insomnia
solving the problems of the world.

When I say *world*, I mean distance:
me on one bank, you on the other,
a rushing between that could be fire.

When I say *fire*, I mean I need
a slash and burn, ash circling
in the black willows, a singing.

2. AS IT HAPPENED NARRATION

The dog (impatient, loafing) drops his ball
and drops his ball and, sick of my staring, eats
the millipedes that crawl out of the closet,
where they are fucking and fucking nightly.

I decide to take the dog for a walk
and, as we enter the park, think,
I bet this buffel grass was planted above
a trove of fossils and graves, which is right

about when I see the five screech owls unfurl
and stretch. Long-lost cousins of the hawk,
dusk hunters, they sweep through the willows, scan
a field of asters and the gristle weeds.

3.1. RECALL: NOSTALGIA

The sun had been the perfect past
of sun, before the earth was peopled and unpeopled and light coursed
    through its valley of hours
and fell with matches and withering.

From the blockhouse lookout,
the ice rink sank its love songs into the hills around, and the elms,
    locusts, and hornbeams
were listening, each grove
switching, each tousled branch sifting north wind up along the paths
    running their tracks,
cement and sand—all
these songs converging on
the old house of stone.

Like any spring, the molting
everywhere made eyewells pulse. Often nothing stayed still so I
    would stand until I could
separate clicking squirrels
from seed pods falling on slate.

I recall you weren't there
and the dog was, but when I saw the owls and heard their machine
    whirs, I remembered we were
both early adults, two
children who could talk to adults because they know the bodies
    (hamster, human) will stiffen—
eight shushed in a year
I knew we're meant together.

3.2. RECALL: A NOTE ON FALSE MEMORIES

Atoms are not things, they are tendencies. Particles can be in multiple
places at once—easier for a mind to fix them, say, at the park, having
an epiphany. It is true at the subnuclear level we can be understood to
be one: owls, pines, you, I. It is also true that addictions, say, to solitary
revelings, are possible because we have dreamt of nothing better.

3.4. Recall: Gaps in the Record

Around that time I was reading things like:
The knights in the wood knew the moon never
would cure their super-sensual loneliness,
and writing things like: Once in a while I let
go of the brake, the late-night conductor

said easily. Or was that a previous spring?

4. On Recording

No logical system is free
from inconsistency. If one
has reeked of box wine, one
knows this, or if you've had
the woods stuck in your eye.

Add to that that nothing existent
is measurable except
by slight collisions and flitterings
imperceptible to senses,
Henry Adams said, more or less.

This is not to speak of facts
(gilt-trimmed talons, for instance)
left out. The issue with the you:
she's not the she exactly—more
a sum of missing gears.

In *Minimalism Simplified*
Einstein says *now* depends on where
you stand. Thus for the you
who has a bulse of flints always
on her person, the one

here and not here, who listens
to her old patients rattle
on for hours and listens
to her old man rattle on

on owls and all the missing letters:
I is such a narrow one,
so singular, so flimsy,
but *we* still means enough.

L'HEURE VERTE

Mornings you are the ruins of yourself,
Green calcite. Where the eyes dried,
Two black rooks lie nesting in the grooves
Worn smooth by thousands of hands
Groping toward the brilliant ocean.
Near the bottom of your hollow mouth,
Your cut tongue gathers lizard scales
Like a sunken bucket in an algal well.
Well, well. You've learned your lesson
This time, haven't you? All the monks
Have died, in their single-cell caves
On the mountainside, their rice-bowls
Overturned. What you so often think
Belongs to you, does not belong to you at all.

FOR LOVE TO EXIST

We must cross the borders of the city.
Cheers. Unhanded, all the women
Must toss their veils behind them,

Smiling. Cheese. For love to exist,
We must take our love by storm,
Our lips reforming all the famous promises.

I will never leave you. I will occupy
Your heart. When it gets hot, I will distribute
Orange crush from the back of a truck.

For love to exist, an army of philanthropists
Must form a phalanx of benevolence,
Extending in each hand a fist of violets.

For love to exist, we must love love rather more
Than what we love, we must recruit lovers today
Who will salute to love on the anniversary of love.

In return, we promise we will harvest love
In the form of a tryst, a mushroom, or a cloud
Above a field: two fronts waiting to embrace.

FIRE

more the idea of the flame than the flame,
as in: the flame

of the rose petal, the flame of the thorn
the sun is a flame, the dog's teeth

flames

———

to be clear: with the body,

captain, we can do as we wish, we can do
as we wish with the body

but we cannot leave marks—capt'n I'm
trying to get this right

———

the world's so small, the sky's so high
we pray for rain it rains, we pray for sun it suns

we pray on our knees, we move our lips
we pray in our minds, we clasp our hands

our hands look tied before us

I remember, capt'n, something, it didn't happen, not
to me—this guy, I knew him by

face, I don't remember his
name, one night
he's walking home from a party, a car it

clipped him, for hours he
wandered, dazed, his family, his
neighbors, with flashlights they

searched, all night, the woods, calling out
his name

———

here's the part, capt'n, where I try to tell a story
as if it were a confession: once,

in elementary school, I was hiding out
on damon rock, lighting
matches & letting them drop to the leaves

below—little flare-

ups, flash fires—a girl wandered
down the path, she just

stood there, watching the matches fall from my hand—

———

capt'n, I'm trying to be precise: hot

day, a cage in the sun, a room without

air, the mind-bending heat, the music

a flame—hey
metallica hey britney hey airless hey fuse, I

don't know how it happened, I was perched far
above, I offered her a match
to pull down her pants—one match, her
hairless body, hey

little girl, I dropped it unlit.

I didn't know what it was I was looking at.

— — —

hey capt'n I don't know if I'm allowed
hey capt'n years ago I'm walking

down a road one drunk night, even now I
wonder—sometimes still I

imagine—was I hit by a bus, am I stumbling am I

dazed, this

dream this confession, hey
little girl is yr daddy home, hey capt'n hey

sir am I making any sense?

— — —

the boy stood on the burning deck, stammering
elocution, wait—
the boy stood in the burning cage, stammering
electrocution, no—the boy stood in the hot-hot room

stammering I did stammering I did stammering I
did stammering I did stammering everything you say I did
I did.

———

hey metallica hey britney hey airless hey fuse
hey phonograph hey hades hey thoughtless hey

———

capt'n this room is on fire
capt'n this body will not stop burning
capt'n oh my captain this burning has become a body
capt'n oh my captain this child is ash
capt'n oh my captain my hands pass right through her
capt'n oh my captain I don't know what it is I'm looking at

———

it's important to be precise, to say what
I know—

the sun is fire, the center of the earth
is fire, yr mother's cunt is

fire, an airless flame, still, still, I don't know why
she pushed me out, this cold-cold furnace, we all

were pushed, a rim of light around our heads, she
gave a kick, sent us crawling

out, toward the flame, toward the pit, the flaming
pit, yr lover's

cunt, the flame her tongue, the flame

a thorn

———

every day, capt'n, sir, captain, I was
left, a child, after school, I was alone, I found

a match, under the sink I found a can, a spray
can, *ly-sol dis-infectant*, it made a

torch, I was careful the flame didn't
enter the can, I knew it

would explode, somehow I knew, I'm
trying to be clear, sir—the flame

shot across the room, then it was gone

PHEROMONE

Sky electric after this midsummer
drought, but a day of rain

won't be enough. The clover won't return,
or the nights we slept the fields,

clinging to their petals. The keeper clips

the grass outside the hive,
& the old guard, full of venom,
prods us to attack. We stud her suit with stingers

until we hang dead from the netting,
until she becomes the word *enemy*, her arms

flailing. Jagged light

surrounds us, her daughter
waits in their truck, screams, the air
brightens. From this distance

she looks no bigger than a possum
as she mouths the word *mother*.

WORKER (LOST)

Half-filled mugs of beer

sour in the sun, thick with
corpses. The busboy flings them

into the sewer. My sisters

have scattered far, to the city
& markets, drunk on
cut watermelon. All I knew

was nectar,
the long tongues of wildflowers, an orchid

that swallowed me whole. Nothing
to return to, the queen dead, I
pressed against her until her eyes

hung empty. Afterwards,

the hive full of strangers,
none remained
precisely me, none

I would die for.

LAUREL TO THE SUN GOD, APOLLO

When you raged, I knew the reason.
Not that I smiled over fondly at others,
bared the tops of my breasts
or failed to close my knees in company.
It was my separateness,
the bonds that tied me to my mother,
that denied complete surrender.

Now rooted, boughs stretching skyward,
no point of entry in bole or crotch,
unmoved by tempests or searing ardors,
I feel your gold head resting in my branches
and the leaves sing.

THE ODDITY PROBLEM

With proper rewards, subjects learn
to distinguish any "odd" member of a set
from those that are similar.
—"learning theory," *Encyclopaedia Britannica*

exclude fatigue. drugs. alterations
in motives. the disturbed. ideal
subjects do not appear all at once.

like first-aid manuals. no need
for the aging. or brain damaged.
the old habits. our most bandaged.

the simplest animals. frogs for example.
barometers in a swamp. dying.
dangling all day till dead. waiting for

the reflexes of habit. now lost.
acid soup of memory. now still.
green carcass on white labcoat.

sometimes the rats forget. which
is it. obtain reward. avoid punishment.
obtain punishment. avoid reward. reward

punishment. avoid reward. obtain.
obtain now less familiar. like one's name.
after the distraction of a maze.

precise skills become routine. almost
habit. most pigeons discriminate colors
humans cannot see. we look the same

to them. even geese know what round is.
what triangularity means. after training.
after pacing into the corners of the cage.

solution to a breakthrough: never hunt
for familiars. the x. or any reassurance.
the end of the march means continue.

expect a response. harbor for one.
make reward an essential condition.
leave the pigeons and geese to sea.

TWO SKETCHES OF HORSES

As for the three horses
Standing under the tree when
Lightning hit it,
One was old,
The horse I rode as a kid.
One was a colt I was starting.
One was beautiful, a gunmetal
Blue roan, and way too crazy to ride.
One by one I put
A rope around their necks
And dragged them behind the truck
To a low spot, where scavengers
Could do their work in peace.
The crazy one—that was
The first time she'd had
A rope around her neck.
I went back a year later.
Coyotes hadn't scattered their bones,
But the three skeletons were clean
So it was like
Three horses running together,
White ghost horses running
Lying down across the
Surface of the earth.

Tonight a beautiful girl,
Blond hair loose about her shoulders,
Walks out into the pasture
With a bag of carrots.
The wildflowers printed on
Her summer dress match
(Or close enough)
The real wildflowers in the field.
The butterflies stitched
On her cowboy boots
Match the butterflies
That rise where she walks
And settle back into the tall grass
Where she passes.
Six yearling colts come up
To nuzzle her and get their carrots.
Beyond her, snowy mountains
And the sunset detonating
A tree shaped cloud.
I watch from the doorway,
And for a minute, maybe longer,
Everything
That threatens us
Threatens to save us.

BOLSHEVESCENT

You stand far from the crowd, adjacent to power.
You consider the edge as well as the frame.
You consider beauty, depth of field, lighting
to understand the field, the crowd.
Late into the day, the atmosphere explodes
and revolution, well, revolution is everything.
You begin to see for the first time
everything is just like the last thing
only its opposite and only for a moment.
When a revolution completes its orbit
the objects return only different
for having stayed the same throughout.
To continue is not what you imagined.
But what you imagined was to change
and so you have and so has the crowd.

DONALD HALL

POND AFTERNOONS

When early July's
Arrival quieted the spring's black flies,
We spent green afternoons
Stretched on the moss
Beside dark Eagle Pond, and heard across
Its distances the calling of the loons.

The days swam by,
Lazy with slow content and the hawk's cry.
We lost ambition's rage,
Forgot it all,
Forgot Jane Kenyon, forgot Donald Hall,
And sleepily half-glanced at a bright page.

Day after day
We crossed the flaking railroad tracks and lay
In the slant August sun
To nap and read
Beneath an oak, by the pond's pickerelweed.
Then acorns fell: These days were almost done.

THE TOUCHING

The months of absence hurry.
In sleep I touch her skin
And wake in the stain of dawn, in fury
Once more to know
It was her pillow
That mimicked the touch of a dead woman.

ELEGY IN INDIA INK

"Le suicide offre tous les avantages: c'est raffiné, c'est chargé de sens, c'est fin-de-siècle."
[Suicide offers every advantage: it's refined, it's filled with meaning,
   it's fin-de-siècle].

—TONINO BENAQUISTA, *Saga*

I.
Before the traffic of human lives made headlines
(opening inside page of a Monday *New York Times*)
four virgins of the village of Bhilai,
inland from the Bay of Bengal,
not far from Bangladesh or Nepal, in India,
on the seventh of April, sisters,
committed suicide.

Aged sixteen to twenty-four,
Minakshi, Meena, Hemlata, and Kesar
wrote a note on lined paper that they left near the door:
We four sisters are fed up with our lives.

They started early the night before.
They pooled their money and bought some cakes.
They stayed up late playing card games and tricks.
They played with words.
They stayed awake.
They ate sweets until they were sick.
They fell asleep on the concrete floor.
One, two, three, four:
the early hours quickly passed.
One, two, three, four:
they hung themselves from rafters with long scarves.

II.

The calligraphy of bodies in midair,
dim in the dusty light,
spelled out the sisters' last wish.
Something still lived in those dark silhouettes,
in the alphabet of limbs and in the stiff gray lips,
something desperate and deliberate,
impossible for the illiterate,
something illegible, difficult at first, faint,
then, on second glance, was quite clear
and impossible to erase:
Minakshi, Meena, Hemlata, Kesar.
It was their names, their names that lived there.

III.

In the West, suicide is linked to mental illness—depression,
     dementia, suicidal tendencies.
Schizophrenia, neurasthenia, panic disorders, the willies.
In the West, suicide is all in the head.

In the East, they say that suicide is perhaps a different malaise—
     social, economic, political.
A question of caste, of debt, of ancestry, of industry.
One of arranged marriages, dowries, *paneer*, chutney, education,
     elephants, offspring.
Of sacred cows with six legs, of an ancient society in a new century.
Of something else, something indistinct and obscure:
the shadows of so many women and their weight in the third world.

IV.

Perhaps our word *suicide* contains an answer to their death:
s, a thinly curved consonant escaping into air,
u, the you, the incriminating vowel,
the twins, *i*, that cancel one another out,
cancel out the self,
the sluice and wave of *c*,
d, soft thud of tongue against gums, penultimate

before the demise, the *coup de grace*, mum—
the final, silent *e*.
But this is all occidental.
Their suicide was premeditated, oriental.

V.
On the palms of their hands,
on the soles of their feet,
on the walls of their house,
they wrote their names.
Blue ink stained deep
skin, smooth and pale as parchment,
marked walls discolored with dirt,
and in few words spelled out their suicide note,
their final, desperate hope:
Minakshi, Meena, Hemlata, Kesar.

IMPLICATIONS FOR MODERN LIFE

The ham flowers have veins and are rimmed in rind, each petal a little meat sunset. I deny all connection with the ham flowers, the barge floating by loaded with lard, the white flagstones like platelets in the blood-red road. I'll put the calves in coats so the ravens can't gore them, bandage up the cut gate &; when the wind rustles its muscles, I'll gather the seeds and burn them. But then I see a horse lying on the side of the road and think *You are sleeping, you are sleeping, I will make you be sleeping.* But if I didn't make the ham flowers, how can I make him get up? I made the ham flowers. Get up, dear animal. Here is your pasture flecked with pink, your oily river, your bleeding barn. Decide what to look at and how. If you lower your lashes, the blood looks like mud. If you stay, I will find you fresh hay.

MINOTAUR, NO MAZE

At the DMV Robo-Boy presents his hands. It makes you wonder. Why would they bother to engrave on each palm a life line (deep and long), a head line (joined to his life line meaning he has "a cautious, sometimes fearful nature") and a heart line (faint and dotted, that figures) and forget to give him fingerprints? The woman looks down at the form. She has little epaulettes of dandruff on each shoulder. "Is there a reason the subject cannot be fingerprinted? An amputation? Current injury? Other, please explain." She looks up and then back down again. And so Robo-Boy falls under the category of "other" again. Nervously he picks at his wrist with his fingernail (fingernails he has) until a bit of beige flakes off and he can see his silver undercoat glinting through. His mother keeps a little can of Skinspray #439 for touch-ups in her bedside table drawer along with her pearls and her vitamins. Once she broke a bottle of foundation in her bag and when he looked inside it seemed lined with her skin. It pleased and scared him—he half-expected a pair of eyes to blink open above the zipper mouth of the inside pocket. Instant baby sister. The woman is signaling for her supervisor—first subtly with her eyebrows, but soon she's making huge loops and whorls with her arms. Robo-Boy looks at her desk, her phone, her black coffee mug—there are fingerprints everywhere, little gray mazes that all lead back to her big gold name tag, which reads HOW MAY I HELP? I'M (and then scrawled in smeared ink) Janice.

NOVEMBER 3, 2004

I cut out the eyes of a politician.
They were blue eyes. The pupils, blown wide.
& over my own eyes
I glued them, thinking, Now I can see
how utterly weak I am. Yes,
weakness spread thickly—numbingly—
to every nerve, every nerve ending.
I thought: Any second my own dog,
my ancient, bald dog
will rise & urinate on my foot. Any second
you will walk into the room
& hurl my well-hidden Box of Weakness
against my chest. You will grab
The Weakness between my legs
& order me to assume
a certain weak position . . . I will crawl,
on my hands & knees, out into the weak-feeling air,
air so weak I can hardly breathe it, out
onto the weakly lit street
where a measly, flea-infested sparrow
will land on my head
and, as if someone pulled a string, shit
down the side of my cheek. Weeping
bird shit will surely be my weakest moment.
But because I am unable to defend myself
from this act of violence, because
I am so profoundly, intensely weak,
I will perform the weakest possible act:
I will sit down in the middle of an intersection,
an intersection full of idling, large cars

& crisp, powerful pedestrians,
pedestrians freshly emerged
from vacuum-packed canisters,
& pour gasoline over my head,
& gaze up at the clean white object of a gathering cloud.

THE BLUE STROM

Never let the ink
of biographers touch you,
but if it happens
learn what you can
of their witchcraft.
It will be useful
should you ever find yourself
without linen.
I would never have risen
above backwoods,
bow-tied Superintendent
or circuit judge had I not studied
the alchemy of metaphor.
There are maybe two dozen gaps
in a given sentence.
Never mistake silence
for death or obedience.
Just because an anthem can't be heard
over the bluegrass
of lawn parties and amphitheaters
doesn't mean it can't be sung.
If you stand on the porch
of the state house on a Sunday
you will hear the great flag
of the confederacy.
On some occasions
you may have to lower an earlobe
to the tongue whipping in the mouth
of the one Negro servant
who remains when everything else

is burned. Avoid anyone,
even your secretary, who talks
openly about revenge.
Master the filibuster,
for it will wear out the sentries
of heaven. Cultivate horticulture.
Marry after forty. Outlaw basketball.
Outlaw school buses. Outlaw
the manufacturing of transistors.
Outlaw jive-talk and rhythm.
If you intend to be re-elected
certain moods must be abolished,
it goes without saying. Remember
your duty. If you must apologize,
let it be in a language no one comprehends.

TO MICK JOYCE IN HEAVEN

I.
Kit-bag to tool-bag,
Warshirt to workshirt—
Out of your element
Among farmer in-laws,
The way you tied sheaves
The talk of the country,
But out on your own
When skylined on scaffolds—
A demobbed Achilles
Who was never a killer,
The strongest instead
Of the world's stretcher-bearers,
Turning your hand
To the bricklaying trade.

2.
Prince of the sandpiles,
Hod-hoplite commander
Watching the wall,
Plumbing and pointing
From pegged-out foundation
To first course to cornice,
Keeping an eye
On the eye in the level
Before the cement set:
Medical orderly,
Bedpanner, bandager
Transferred to the home front,
Rising and shining
In brass-buttoned drab.

3.
You spoke of "the forces."
Had served in the desert,
Been strafed and been saved
By courses of blankets
Fresh-folded and piled
Like bales on a field.
No sandbags that time.
A softness preserved you.
You spoke of sex also
Talked man to man,
Took me for granted:
The English, you said,
Would do it on Sundays
Upstairs, in the daytime.

4.
The weight of the trowel,
That's what surprised me.
You'd life its lozenge-shaped
Blade in the air
To sever a brick
In a flash, and then twirl it
Fondly and lightly.
But whenever you sent me
To wash it and dry it
And you had your smoke,
Its iron was heavy,
Its sloped-angle handle
So thick-spanned and daunting
I needed two hands.

5
"To Mick Joyce in Heaven"—
The title just came to me,
Mick, and I started
If not quite from nowhere,
Then somewhere far off:
A bedroom, bright morning,
A man and a woman,
Their backs to the bedhead
And me at the foot.
It was your first leave,
A stranger arrived
In a house with no upstairs,
But heaven enough
To be going on with.

JANE HIRSHFIELD

THE STORY

"Do you ever—"

my weeping friend asked.

I lied and said yes

and invented a story,

a fate I would now

have also to live through,

because like a bride

I had promised myself to its hands.

SIR MUHAMMED IQBAL

Translated by Rafiq Kathwari

HIMALAYA
for Lucie Brock-Broido

O Himalaya, tell of that time when man first lay
in your lap. O let me imagine that dawn
unstained by red. Run backward, cycle of day
and night, ancient eras a moment in your lifetime.
You are a poem whose first verse is the sky.
Your bright turbans dazzle the Pleiades.
Lightning across your peaks sends black tents wandering
above the valley. The wind polishes the trembling mirrors
at your hem. Streams cascade down your forehead,
your cheeks quiver. As morning air cradles intoxicated
roses and the leaves are silenced by the rose gatherer's wrist,
so speech is silenced in the roar of falling water.

PETER KLINE

MINOTAUR

You wound a ball of twine around my eyes, then pinned
the end between my fingers.

You gowned me in white tissue
like a hothouse nectarine.

The furtive door at last unbarred, I was
amazed at the garden's suggestion

throating from vining flower-walls
in breaths that quickened with mine.

How long I lingered beneath
sun awnings and a stone-and-mortar sky,

only you know. For when I found the throne room
festooned with pelvis bones,

the twin-fingered god on whose nether lip I hung
a kiss, a crape-gartered barb,

was you—you the pursued, yours
the bull's head draped with fragrant lash-black hair.

A TENDENCY TOWARD MYSTICISM

All I wanted was to take you somewhere,
to be lonely. I could never stand it.

Somewhere out of here. That was forever
ago or yesterday; wherever the voice

stretches from, from mist, from an idea,
it ends with the moon swallowing trees

& depositing them on houses, trains,
gazebos, a pond of thin ice. I couldn't

understand, had other worries, wasn't
interested in folklore & self-mythologizing.

I didn't think anything. I pulled myself
together, like a man once on a cliff,

then walking away. I could feel my stomach,
was always glad it was over. There will be

a last conversation; the purpose to get
close enough to touch you. We will

shed under separate skins. I can do this.
Say the things you say. Say hello. Hello.

I can do this. There is a growing
apprehension that my peers are listening.

I enjoyed our silence, was suited for it.
I am not cynical. I am a man with two

feet on the ground. I drink coffee, smoke;
am not a coward. I can only report

what I know, like that man standing
on a cliff. This is a sophisticated thought.

The human body wants desperately to die
& does. I had said what I never meant

to say. Please stay with me.

pearsap

I

juice of a pear fresh
plucked from a tree
ripe with far-off fire

II

anjou	bijou
bosc	cosset
comice	promise
bartlett	whet
clapp	palate
seckel	suckle
nellis	nuzzle
forelle	always
sun	sunned

III

broken syllables
of caught light
dappled on our tongues

IV

on my kitchen table
the bartlett pears sit

like small friendly gnomes
leaning toward my skillet

before i peel them
i admire the skins

they are the color of
what it is to await

transformation

V

unwept longing for
even one right-weighted word
so true filtered

VI

sun-struck
    these pears
    wandered wild
stuck on branches
    but tree-free to dream
            drunk

            fingered
                gasping
                    sky-sighted
            earth-found
to my kitchen
        where i keep trying
                to learn
                    to mend
ill-thought-out
        recipes   how to
            trust my senses
                improvise
        both hands   laugh
            as i wrestle
                with the bartletts
            over who makes
                who fell? I flew!
                    dessert

VII

breath-nursed creatures
that we are   we long
to have our mouths filled

VIII

sought tastebud tongue
lip chin chest
clavicle sternum past
sex stout legs breathless
to the ground where even
the worms turn earth
in abandoned delight

HEAT OF DAY

Blocked by a garbage can, I could see just
the ribs and back. *Albino*, I thought, then,
Can't be; the fur surely orange, but pale,
pale, girded with white so cleanly I thought,
Evil. The spine curled under, the tail
straightened and held. The darker tip
quivered with a mind of its own. Only then,
the crouch: I had looked away an instant,
and it blindsided me; no, it swerved toward me
and clamped, like teeth in meat—
the legs wound themselves down, springs
cranked a breath's push at a time.
I felt each notch in my shoulders.
All I could think: *Look at that, Look
at that*, seeing a phantom in the sculpted
hindquarters, a pair of cornered eyes
with all we know dawning on them.

FEBRUARY 28

God is the cloud that
travels with my caravan,
Bessie Smith is in my living room
singing "Do Your Duty," and
I may look like a gas station attendant
but my name is Jackson Pollock
and I'm the Big Bang Professor
of theoretical physics
at Southern Comfort University,
and as a good citizen
of this fading century
whose rules of sexual engagement
were laid down by the Marquis de Sade
I know I am responsible for all I see
which I have organized
into cities and chambers
as one might organize the sea

HALLELUJAH BLACKOUT[5]

The phonographs of hades in the brain
Are tunnels that rewind themselves, and love
A burnt match skating in a urinal
                              —HART CRANE

Night spreads open like this
Don't stop—the cicadas
Droning their susurrus to the sun

If he needs more—
If the wind heaves and grows
If nothing is forgotten or rearranged

The milky blue of midnight does not stop
For blossoming. For our thanks and less
The milky blue of midnight does not stop
A walker hums his bad rollicking heaven
The milky blue of midnight does not stop
Two-by-fours crack away from a birch

Why does the wet grass, the days washed steps
Erase the rabbit pillaging the lilacs
A rabbit pillaging the lilacs stops
To recognize you, why does the wet grass

My friends, the sutured
Light of the sleepless stings
The city is so tired, so breathless

Tomorrow will sickly grow
Explain to me why this house
Is and I will groan and lean, yearning
A bloody nose, a pow-pow of fresh paint

LOOK CLOSE

Rain is holding its breath—water-damaging
The oatmealy clouds and you must want

To be the stranger of swollen doorways,
The specialist who cannot carve my insides

Enough. When you think midnight,
Do you taste hot honey and water

Or muffler rust? When you hear thunder,
Remember the bowling balls herding

Around the buckled wood of your mother's home.
Bathroom light, womb-bright, the six-packs

Are slow tonight. There is a car smashing
Around my chest. Do you hear the breath

Of the waiting? It doesn't matter how
Many times we prick our tongues and touch.

BEI LING

Translated by Willis Barnstone and Denis Mair

TIME LIKE A FALLEN HORSE

When time like a fallen horse
Bursts open, one instant a lifetime
The gigantic horse's head
Wind . . . fetters its throat

All faces are facing apocalyptic times
Pull together, a kiss resembling steel
Last cleansing in a dry night
Riddle, penetrate the whole body

DOG DAYS

Cruising potholed streets from dusk
to dawn—bottles of Absolut rolling
on a backseat floor where dreams

went up in smoke. Barbecued ribs
transporting us from freezer burn
to voracious mouths yawing wide

for tinder gathered by rosy campfire
girls—stalks of corn "knee-high
by the Fourth of July" we used to say

with all of our fuses lit—the future
halfway up the sky as bottle rockets
turned the neighbor's house to ash.

DON'T ASK, DON'T TELL

Ours was a nascent science
piling up under the night sky's

psychopomp—his uniform

a door into the supra-personal:
was in some barracks under

the drill sergeant's commands

then slammed into my body
from afar. And what the fuck

were he doing stabbing me

with his sex, me no longer
knowing where I was, if I was.

FEDERICO GARCÍA LORCA

Translated by Pablo Medina and Mark Statman

ODE TO WALT WHITMAN

By the East River and the Bronx
the young men sang, baring their waists
with the wheel, the oil, the hide, and the hammer.
Ninety thousand miners mined silver from the rocks
and the children drew stairwells and perspectives.

But none fell asleep,
none wished to be the river,
none loved the large leaves
or the beach's blue tongue.

By the East River and the Queensboro
the young men wrestled with industry,
and the Jews sold the rose of circumcision
to the faun of the river
and the sky spilled over bridges and rooftops
herds of buffalo pushed by the wind.

But none stopped,
none wished to be a cloud,
none looked for ferns
or the yellow wheel of the drum.

When the moon rises
the pulleys will turn to trouble the sky;
a border of needles will circle memory
and coffins will carry off those who don't work.

New York of filth,
New York of wires and death.

What angel do you carry hidden in your cheek?
What perfect voice will speak the truths of wheat?
Who the terrible dreams of your stained anemone?

Not for one moment, beautiful old Walt Whitman,
have I not seen your beard full of butterflies,
or your corduroy shoulders worn away by the moon,
or your virginal Apollo thighs,
or your voice like a column of ash;
beautiful old man, like the mist,
who cried like a bird
with its sex pierced by a needle.
Enemy of the satyr,
enemy of the vine
and lover of bodies under coarse cloth.
Not for one moment, virile beauty
on mountains of coal, billboards, and railroads,
did you dream of being a river and sleeping like a river
with that comrade who would place in your chest
the small sorrow of an ignorant leopard.

Not for a single moment, macho Adam of blood,
man alone at sea, beautiful old Walt Whitman
because on rooftops,
gathered in bars,
leaving the sewers in bunches,
trembling between the legs of chauffeurs,
or spinning on platforms of absinthe,
the queers, Walt Whitman, are pointing at you.

That one, too! That one! And they hurl themselves
on your chaste and luminous beard
blonds from the north, blacks from the sands,
crowds of cries and gestures
like cats and like snakes,
the queers, Walt Whitman, the queers,
their troubled tears, meat for the whip,
the boot or bite of their masters.

That one, too! That one! Stained fingers
point at the shore of your dream,
when a friend eats your apple
with a slight taste of gasoline
and the sun sings in the navels
of the young men playing under the bridge.

But you weren't looking for scratched eyes,
or the darkest swamp where they submerge the boys,
or the frozen saliva,
or the curved wounds like the belly of a toad
the queers wear in cars and on terraces
while the moon whips them through the corners of terror.

You looked for a nude that might be a river
and moan in the flames of your hidden equator,
bull and dream that join the wheel with seaweed,
father of your agony, camellia of your death.

Because it's fitting that a man not seek for his pleasure
in the bloody jungles of tomorrow morning.
The sky has beaches where life is avoided
and there are bodies that shouldn't repeat themselves at dawn.

Agony, agony, dream, ferment, and dream.
This is the world, friend, agony.
The dead decompose below the clocks of the cities,
war passes weeping with a million gray rats,

the rich give their lovers
small illuminated deaths,
and life is not noble, or good, or sacred.

If he wishes, man can guide his desires
through a vein of coral or naked blue sky.
Tomorrow the lovers will be stone and Time
a breeze that walks sleeping through the branches.

And so, I don't raise my voice, old Walt Whitman,
against the boy who writes
a girl's name on his pillow,
or against the young man who dresses like a bride
in the darkness of his closet,
or the solitary men in the casinos
who drink with disgust the water of prostitution,
or the green men who leer, who love
other men and burn their lips in silence.
But I will against you, queers of the cities,
of tumescent flesh and filthy thought,
mothers of mud, harpies, dreamless enemies
of the Love that delivers crowns of joy.

Against you always, who give young men
drops of dirty death with bitter poison.
Against you always,
Fairies of North America,
Pájaros of Havana,
Jotos of Mexico,
Sarasas of Cádiz,
Apios of Seville,
Cancos of Madrid,
Floras of Alicante,
Adelaídas of Portugal.

Queers of the world, assassins of doves!

Slaves of women. Bitches of their dressing rooms,
open in the plazas with a fan-like fever
or ambushed in stiff landscapes of hemlock.

No mercy! Death
pours out of your eyes
and clusters gray flowers on the shores of filth.
No mercy! Look!
Let the confused, the pure,
the classical, the chosen, the supplicants
shut on you the doors of the bacchanal.

And you, beautiful Walt Whitman, sleep on the shores of the
    Hudson
with your beard pointed toward the pole and your hands open.
Soft clay or snow, your tongue is calling
comrades to watch over your bodiless gazelle.
Sleep: nothing remains.
A dance of walls shakes the prairies
and America sinks into machines and tears.
I want the strong airs of deepest night
to remove the flowers and letters from the arch where you sleep
and a black boy to announce to the white golden ones
the arrival of the kingdom of grain.

THE SMALLEST WOMAN IN THE WORLD WHO ONCE POSED ON THE LAP OF THE RICHEST MAN IN AMERICA CONSIDERS THE BAD DREAMS OF THE TALLEST MAN WHO EVER LIVED

His mother even on tiptoe   no longer can she straighten his tie.
Even when he was a boy   his father inherited his shirts.

Pituitary giant, pathologically tall. Apologetic—

his height is not his fault, he claims. At 22 he'll die
still growing. Foot trouble in Alton, Illinois. Across yoked beds,
his room crowded with him, he dreams perhaps
of Babylon
& Pisa. Gravity,
the master, hums as he collapses.

———

And the anatomists hide   behind far-flung drapes.
Tailors stand on chairs   measuring the horizon

for his wake-wear. Major Atom & Admiral Dot

battle over the territory between his lifeline
& his carpus. Jack schemes. Chandeliers tangle
like flocks of stars charging his hat from all sides

at once. Gog & Magog burly the sea. Slingshot
stones with old testament intentions graze
his periphery,
but it's wartime
when only bombers could tease his reach.

— — —

Every cubit & span of him   measured. Altitude
& inseam. Shoe size 37—   *extremities gross & fragile.*

Weight 21 stone. His chart-lines inexorable. At 7:

the tallest Boy Scout. *Tall Pine*, Minnesotan
Indians name him. Robert Wadlow. Hardly a sideshow
in his suit & tie, he became a shoe-store icon. His adirondackish
rocking chair built to scale is staged center in a back room off
the alley where he takes local questions about his breakfast plate,

his fear of falling down, ceiling fans, how he fits
into voting booths, his
wristwatch band & leg
braces, dropsy, how he climbs narrow stairs.

— — —

And the scientists tribe   to snatch & dissect.
The Great Anatomist,   after the stature

of The Irish Giant, bribes undertakers

to restock his nine-foot coffin with pavement stones. Lurking
in this dream, casting ten-foot shadows, anatomists past
plot to topple the tallest into an aesculapian kettle—the colossal

boiled skeletal,
tagged, immortal,
to be strung up alongside the wee bones of a Sicilian dwarf.

— — —

We live & will die   on opposite sides of the pituitary, opposite
sides of the Atlantic.   From the lap of America, little me

misses my mother in Germany. His mother tiptoes

to exit his dreams, across a tundra laced with redundant humerus,
tibia, phalanges. He pursues, ice worrying his footing. His leg brace
scrapes his leg infectious, unbeknownst. We are not so miraculous
after all. He is no taller than my last breath
which shall rise
as my body hides
in a room crowded with gas. Our combined measurements: history.

OPPENHEIMER ON THE COUCH

First, meaning possession.

Now we have on our hands
this porcupine.
I chase it under the bed
and dream I'm a passenger
on a doomed cruise. The subconscious

has not been warned
about the use of cliché:
sinking ship, it says.

Sometimes I want to steal
but my understanding of loss
prevents me.

Rock between two hard places.

We drowned in our teacups
and woke on a bed of quills.

First, meaning option
not to use
only *wield.*

YOUR CHILDHOOD

I.
Years later, frozen at a curb, atilt before the traffic's
loud blur, preparing to launch into the street deep
with Technicolor chromes and lose myself to the legs
tangling forth, even now, I can spy it limping across
the horizon's tired red that rests its lip just beyond
the farthest line of my vision, can see it scuttle off
into the safety of the softly shadowed mouth of an
alleyway. What's next? Yesterday, the sign it lugged
begged for bus fare. Today, it wears a cast fashioned
from newspaper. Tomorrow, it'll ask if I have change
for a nickel. And tonight, somewhere beneath a soiled
rumple of cardboard spongy with rainwater, lies your
scheming childhood, hatching up more pitiful plans.

II.
Your childhood and I go way back. Remember when
it put its finger down my throat when I got too drunk
to walk? We slipped those tubes of pink lipstick up our
sleeves at the shopping mall, we chewed Nicorette while
smoking. I picked it up hitchhiking: its mouth tugged on
a joint as it bragged that it wanted you dead. It got off
wherever I planned to head, said anywhere was where
it planned to end up. Though it never paid for gas, it
knew a trick or two, thought I wasn't looking as it picked
through my purse, and later fingered lovingly my driver's
license. Your childhood wants my childhood, makes out
with my yearbook photo, jacks off to my high school
journal; it comes to love my parents more than I do.

III.
Your childhood turns up viscous in my soup, floats
its pale residue of congealed bacon fat, seals every
meal's surface. Saying *I'm not hungry* translates into
you don't know what it means to go hungry. Standing
in the grocery store's checkout line, it's aghast I'm
buying boneless chicken breasts. It would have me
strip down, flinch beneath the fluorescence, offer up
every last inch of my clothing. Marching up to gather
my garments into its arms, it announces that I'll find
them at the Salvation Army, then strides out between
the electric doors muttering that *some people don't
know how good they have it.* Even when forced to eat
dog food, your childhood was never so ungrateful.

IV.
Your childhood prying open a can, your childhood
waking you because it's afraid of the dark. For years.
Of the yellowing polar bear at that dank zoo which will
not stop banging its head against the concrete floe of
its habitat, you alone know the briny depths of its woe.
Once, your school sent a letter home stating it'd found
you *gifted.* Your mother crumpled it up. The ranging
plains, the dust-strewn land on which you grew. How
could anyone know what it was to grow up as you? If
it had its way, your childhood would smother her, heft
her to a rank ravine's devouring grasses. Hate's her
opium. You don't mind when your voice makes a face
flinch. Maybe you like it. Your childhood's seen to that.

WEATHERWORN

The air was closer than a terrarium's

where bits of transplanted green moss thrive

causing beads of moisture to grow like tears

upon the glass, then slowly descend the sides—

a small tide, unable to stop or wipe away.

The sky cohered in a charcoal canopy

oppressing the flinty stands of paralyzed fir

and song-spent birds. The fountain's naiad looked

tired of balancing the loaded atmosphere

on two slim marble hands—a noble gesture.

Over the world's back a wheel of thunder groaned.

Whether I paced my breathless room or parched lawn

driven by heat, longing for rain,

I held your body's fierce proximity at bay.

Translated by Wendy Burk

NIGHT (QUERULOUS)

Castrating mind, close-mouthed mind,
quasi-calculation, quasi-quality
climbing chain-link
quietly chipping
cracked concrete
chip by chip
by custom.
What changes?
What chastens my mind,
what clamors to cut
and connives quarrels,
creating: cavalry
in consequent corpse;
charging as coltish curls collapse,
collapsing close to countless castle chimeras
that I craved contiguous,
I craved cross and Calvary:
my curtailed cursive that cuts off here,
my curtailed mind that carries on
calmly mutual.

AT THE WIDENING OF A WAR

Everyone was frightened of the sky.

Each night, Mars emerged at the zenith.
A bleb of pure rage tore off the Sun.

For days, the living and the dead
hung in the air like dust
whirled aloft from tired roads.

The fuselage of a lobster lay abandoned.

The Isles of the Blest were receding
to their sailing distances
and the gunfire of tourist shoes was stilled.

Sports stadiums and crowds loomed from another age.

The blow struck now
would be weaker than the blow withheld.

Translated by Paul Muldoon

ODE TO A HARE-BOY

In the light of autumn
and the open road,
the boy
holds up in his hands
not a blossom
nor a lantern
but a dead hare.

The automobiles scan
the freezing camber,
no faces showing
from behind
windshields,
their eyes
of iron,
their ears
set against everything,
their gear-teeth quick
as flashes of lightning,
skidding
towards the sea and the cities
while an autumn-
boy
with a hare,
standoffish
as a thistle,
hard
as a flint,
raises
there
a hand

to the shudder-sighs
of the cars.

Nobody
slows down.

They're dun-dullish,
the high ridges,
the hills
the color of a puma
on the run,
violet
now
the silence,
and like
two embers,
two
black
diamonds,
the eyes
of the hare-boy,
now
two points
set
on a knife,
two little black blade-tips,
the eyes
of the boy
who's all at a loss,
offering up his hare
to the huge
autumn
of the open road.

"YES, WE HAVE NO BANANAS"

was really stolen from Handel's *Messiah*.
It was proven: a lawsuit   and broken pencils.
Fakirs who lie   on beds of nails
        often hold   umbrellas. The pain rains.
A two-inch thick steel cable   snaps
from   the munching   of white ants.
            Sometimes   there is a line
    of ants   across the linoleum   leading
to my dog's   food dish.   And what if
        it was white? Such a heady line   of icing
vibrating   in summer heat! Like cupcakes left too long
        on a picnic table.   Technically
any whale   that washes up   on the shores
of Manhattan   belongs to Trinity Church.
    I know a Sherpa   who patches
            the soles of his feet
with a darning needle and string. I like
    how he is self-aware of self-repair
Wouldn't we all   have belly stitches
            from laughing   too long at the table?
    When   the poet's body   is shredded,
will the head go on singing?

BACH'S *INVENTIONS*

From behind me music starts flowing.
A slight pull on my spine; my fingers
Remember which keys to touch
In what order, and there is no piano.
What's left me is a mind like a blind
Sheet on which certain notes lay
Dying. Last night, I dreamed turning
Into a sewing machine—religiously
I pierced holes like vacant words
In a straight line.
                           I forget how to praise
Order while my fingers still remember
The praise they received for hitting
The right chords: the pleasure derived
From within confinement.
                                        Strong coffee
Washes my senses. What twines round
Each movement is a murmur of Glenn Gould
Who can't help but speak to the keys he
Strokes; the mineral response of his piano
Tears the sacred in a sequence of pitches.
Prolong a grace note beyond
Its due. Praise the distance
Of the hammer from the strings.

PAROUSIA

When we were in the same room as the gods
there was little to say.
Do you like twilight? Do you need the touch
of the other's body—the absolute other?
Mostly we stared at their wingtips
which were burnished
and stamped with strange almost-holes.
How could they stand the suffering
of the fly trying to walk
across the sheen and camber
of a brimming Campari glass?
It would happen to us,
but it was they who had to watch
and watching is hardest.
Only a breath away,
they showed no desire to vanish
though the silences that opened
were volatile as the shadows
of the last exhausted dancers.
Which do you prefer—time or lightning?
We could hear the clink
of the chandelier trying to work its way
loose from the vaulted ceiling,
a cello tuning sharp in an inner room,
and curried almonds being gobbled—
that was us, our voracity,
but the gods said nothing:
their politeness is like their love:
glass wall between us and midnight.
We pitied them. It is not safe

on that side of eternity.
Worse than watching is waiting
while the waiters sweep up the party hats
and dark lights of snow
tumble in the immense gilt-framed mirror.

CHICKADEE

Late at night when the house is silent
I'll put down my book and quarter an apple
or put a few slivers of cheese on a piece
of flatbread, and it must be the poverty
of those meals which makes me think
of the departed, like the old German
who used to walk hunched every afternoon
past my window when I was very small
and wave to me, his walrus moustache
yellowed by cigars (back then all the old
men smoked and they lived forever)
which he held in an amber mouthpiece.
No one in my house knew him, but he waved
just the same, and tapped his cane toward
the corner where the cop stood directing
traffic, but stopped long enough to
tip his cap to the old man, as though
it were a Bing Crosby movie and not
a lousy corner in Queens on an eight-lane
boulevard. And I think again of Fat Charley,
his huge head—thin black hair parted down
the middle—floating above his beer stein,
and his terrible jokes—every 4th of July:
"the blessings of liberty for ourselves
and our posteriors"—and again of my father
walking dark tenement streets in Brooklyn,
collecting crumpled bills from the poor
for their small policies, life & casualty.

I'm sick of pity because it's
always self-referential. This morning,
this warm day in March 500 miles from that
corner in the city, I listened to the birds
in the hawthorn—such singing, and snow is
expected—such difficult lives. One chickadee
came close to inspect me, hopping from
branch to branch to get a better view, until
I could see her carpet-tack beak as she
studied me, cool and fearless, this creature
that weighs an ounce, with her merciless
black-bead reptilian eye.

SHARON OLDS

ON THE HEARTH OF THE BROKEN HOME

Slowly fitting my pinky-tip down
into the wild eggshell fallen
from inside the chimney, I feel as if I'm like
a teenage boy in love, allowed
into the beloved's body, like my father
with the girl he loved, who loved him. If he
had married her . . . I lift it up
close to my eye, the coracle dome
hung with ashes, rivered with flicks
of chint, robes of the unknown—only
a sojourner, in our home, where love
was sparrow-netted to make its own
cage, jessed with its jesses, limed
with its radiant lime. And above the tiny
tossed-off cloak of the swift, in the deep
reaches of the old dutch oven, on a bed
of sprung traps, the mice in them
long gone to meltdown, and to maggotmeal,
and wet dust, and dry dust,
there lies another topped shell, smaller,
next to it its doffed skull
tressed with spinneret sludge, speckled with
flue-mash flecks, or the morse of a species,
when I lift it up, its yolk drops out, hard
amber, light coming through it, fringed
in a tonsure of mold and soot. If I ever
dreamed, as a child, of everlasting
love, these were its shoes: one dew-licked
kicked-off slipper of a being now flying, one
sunrise-milk-green boot of the dead,
which I wore, as I dreamed.

WE'RE NOT FARMERS

We've been starving for so long. Our voices echo
       in our bellies, our throats vibrate.
  We milked the cow, then sold it.
   One by one you behead the chickens. I put them in soup
         so the food will last.
   What's left are a few hens and one cock. You take the eggs away.
To forget, we sleep. Putting on pajamas and crawling into bed
   feels like another chore. You grind your teeth in your sleep,
         and I can't.

I dream we're down to one hen—who can't lay eggs.
   She's my friend. You will not spare her, have your needs too.
        I cook
   but don't eat. While you suck the flesh from each wing,
a noise erupts from your mouth. The hen inside you is clucking
         her tongue.
As your stomach swells, she squawks louder, louder
        until she breaks through.
  You dream of rain every night. Our field's barren.
         I'm not sorry.

CECILY PARKS

HOW TO READ A
MACKEREL SKY

Out of the clouds I make
the whirlpool of shipwreck. I make a stampede.

I make dry leaves spinning
away from piles, a house reduced to shingles,

buttermilk curdling
on a linoleum floor. It's easy

to divine undoing—
flood all the unknowns with your fear, tailor

vapor to harbinger,
and lower the billowing sails of your

keeling soul. Loosed
from any charted course, forsake your grip

on the helm as the sky
becomes sea—silver-scaled with mackerel

teeming to every
horizon—and the shingled house around

your heart quakes for the want
of diagrams, equations, plans. That's when

to look for me, swimming
in leaves the size of fish, dismantling

the ocean and spilling
buttermilk across the sky. I'll be gowned

in linoleum, and you'll
hear hoofbeats, love approaching.

Translated by Steven Seymour

ONE TOUCH IN SEVEN OCTAVES

1.

A light touch with a slant
like a first-grader's handwriting, with a tilt:
you brush away a hair from my cheek
with a motion vaguely tender, stretching
my face slightly upward and to the left,
turning me into a doe-eyed geisha.
With a slant, yet in a straight line:
the shortest and the quickest path.

2.

The trick is in the suffixes, diminutive and endearing:
to diminish first, then to caress,
and by caressing to reduce to naught,
and then to search in panic, where can you be?
Have I dropped you into the gap
between the body and the soul?
And all the while you are right here,
in my arms. So heavy, so enormous!

3.

First, cursory caresses, on the surface,
light, a kind of coloratura: crumbs of
pizzicato in spots which seemingly require
a brusque, tempestuous treatment,
then with a bow across the secret strings,
the ones that were not touched at the beginning,
then across the non-existent strings or, more exactly,
the ones we have never suspected of existing.

4.
Are my palms rubbing your shoulders,
or are your smooth shoulders rubbing my palms,
making them drier, sharper, more perfect?
The more repetitive a caress, the more healing it is.
Water slowly grinds stone; caresses
make the body light, chiseled, compact,
the way it wants to be,
the way it once had been.

5.
Who plays blindman's-buff with those aged twenty,
hide-and-seek with those aged thirty?
Love does. Ah, the silky pelts,
the simple rules, the witless stakes!
Is it easy at thirty-five to say goodbye to love?
It is, not for the reasons of great shame involved,
but because there is no spot more tender, rosier,
more concealed than a scar.

6.
Within a hand's reach from the foreskin
is fleshlessness, dense, resonant, boundless.
Touching, because of its nature, takes part
in the mystery of disembodiment.
I am rid of the body, but the shiver stays,
and so do the pain, the joy.
The shiver, the pain, the joy have no fear
that the skin might never reappear.

7.
How tender the sensation of ants racing,
how many shivers in a slow progression!
Some take no less than a full five minutes
to get from one vertebra to the next.
For years a gentle hand has been the trainer
coaxing them to run from one tiny hair
to the next, until the finishing line,
until it is madness, until . . . *Hey,
are you sleeping?*

COGITO ERGO SUM: MIND REELS

I convinced myself that there is nothing
in the world: no lickable sky, no untouched,

no untouchable earth, no windexed minds or
bodies to hold. Wander at will. Keep nothing.

So: I too do not exist? No:
funny bunny, oh no. You do, most of the time,

you do—with bells & whistles & metal
detectors. Were my bones ever made

of glass I might shine them, spark fires
in the sun with filed fingernails & walk

away slowly. I might. But there are times
when memory's dropped, a box of radios

padded with hummingbird down. The next
of it: the mess of it: what spills. Such honesty

with the world is barely acceptable. Sprung
fully uninformed from the belly of a giddy

god: Cogito ego, I mean, I think
I have a cold; wind & obfuscation

will do that to a girl & all I've ever
needed is a clean white hankie—but it's a red

sock, stuck up my silk sleeve that shoots
into the static crowd. Purgatorially

speaking, ambivalence becomes me, wears
my shoe size & buys too small. It gives us something

to consider while walking.
I did. & then I didn't. Did I

eat an ultraviolet peach in November? No:
I stole one in December & left it here for all to see.

TWENTY-FIVE THOUSAND VOLTS

The weird summer of lightning (to be honest) was not a summer, but
    a week
when we sat every night in a far corner of the yard
to watch the silver twitch above our drinks.
It may help to know the sky hardly ever spasms here,
which is why we savored the postscript of nickel,
ions crisping in the deep fry.

The bolts made everything erogenous, the poppies and the pumpkin
    vine—
we could hardly bear to leave our watch post
but we had tickets for the concert at the pier.
And we could not bear to miss the jam-band from our youth,
which we feared discovering lacked talent and looked foolish
in their caveman belt buckles and leather hats.

Whew. That we found in them a soulfulness, an architecture
of tempo changes and chord progressions,
left us relieved. Childishly
we hummed along as the sun got gulped down like a vitamin
and boats of cheapskates gathered on the bay.
When the lightning started, it was fearsome and silent

as usual. We were older, we knew this,
but the past proved not to be all suicide and motorcycle accidents.
Here was proof the music had shown some finesse—
even if it pillaged the discographies of black men from the Delta
it did so honorably, *erotically*, meaning
"that which gathers." So we held hands and drew near.

And the flashes lit us, when they lit us, in platinum flames:
suddenly we saw, at the foot of the bleachers,

a man whose rubber sneaker toe-tips
punctured the darkness as he spun.
He lurched and spun and lurched and fell,
a messenger from the ancient cults,

his stomach's contents strobed ruthlessly
once they splattered on the tarmac. Sky says: *Rise*
but feet say: *Heavy*. Body would say: *Torn in two*
if it weren't already passed out
with all the Good Samaritans busy remembering
the words to the tune about the rambling man. Oh

Bacchus, Dionysus, ye southern rock stars
of antiquity: thank you for shutting the black door
behind which he vanished, so we could resume
holding each other, like two swigs of mouthwash.
Then the brother who was not dead
played us another of our childhood songs.

PLEASURE

This far in—
where to say *the sea*
and mean *impossible*

makes sense,
why not—you can
almost forget

what brought you here,
the water it started with,
a life that has sometimes (admit

this much) seemed mostly
an only half-wanted because
finally unruly

animal you'd once hoped
to change by changing
its name: from *If Only* to

How Did I
to *In Spite of Everything*—
but nothing sticks, that doesn't

have to. Not memory;
not the naming—which, if a form of
remembering, is also

a form of *to own*, possession,
whose lineage
shifts never: traced

far enough, past hope, back across
belief, it ends always
at desire—without which

would there have been
imagination, would
there be folly,

one spreading itself
like a bay tree, the other
a green olive tree in the house

of God?
This far in, sky
is everything. Clouds cross it

like ships,
sheer will, regret
itself cut abruptly

loose. Lovely, when you say so,
—and when you don't.
It was never for you.

D. A. POWELL

LIPSYNC
[WITH A NOD TO LIPPS, INC.]

put your mouth around a juicy candy, coat
with red dye no. 2: *pucker, fucker*.   then blow

out the candles on the cake: that's how
you make believe you're holding a trembling c note

the *la la la* is like licking pussy [see note]

   —note: that night I fell into a pile with incandescent
               bodies, an ocean of womyn lapping the rocks
               said: come down here and be our playtoy

               did.   and diddled.   [or *dawdled?*] as in PLAYBOY
               I slid up into the one who straddled me.   shaved box
               the warm folds of her felt as a man's stubbly chin

               my tongue went into dark places, as a moray eel slips
               funkytown on the hi-fi, I mouthed the lyrics

                        take me, won't you take me
                        take me, won't you take me, &c. —

what phrase lingers in the back of your larynx
snookums, you could swallow me in three gulps: be so assured

if you don't know the tune, mumble *watermelon, hummingbird*
gesture grandly the way you squirmed between my lips

WALK

I pick up a house of skin.
I pick up a silver nutshell,
ragged, like a hobnail, hit
and gaping more brightly for it,
and see how the world provides.
I see trees are lungs all around.
A sliver of tarp plucked from mud
is so blue I fall down,
really fall, not a stumble,
and green fringes up the real sky.
Down here the ground smells like
milk, iron, water. Dust, blood and butter.
I find a cream petal.
The notch in its edge
makes it a bowl with a place for a spoon.
I want scant things, so few
on their nails, hung on a wall,
a scrappy dirt yard with mint in a ramble,
mint's precise bite I crush with my nail
and bring to my mouth
that I might not fly apart, unseen,
oh sharp star of mint, light on in the house
whose roof is my mouth.

BUT YEATS WAS *ASKED* TO WRITE A POEM ABOUT THE WAR

Can you tell the casualty from the cause?
An angular descent of light
and all arose and it was a new year
very like the old year
yet newly named and colder.

Still the light descended, eight minutes
from the sun, more or less, a gift.

We opened our dictionaries for the morning
service, and some intoned the definitions,
and some the parts of speech, but the wary
huddled in shadow
mumbling etymologies

(*Romanic-speaking peoples, who were obliged
to avoid the Latin* bellum *on account of its formal
coincidence with* bello- *beautiful, found no nearer
equivalent in Teutonic than* werra)

rituals seem funny to the young
who have no need for
talismans against the return of old time
which no one really remembers, dismembered
as it must be upon its tattering return, a turn
against return. But such very forgetting
is power and danger
and anyway this is a new year when
we kiss and make up.

(werran, *whence modern G.* wirren, *wk. vb.*
to confuse, perplex; the earlier vb. survives
in verworren *ppl.a.*, confused, *f. Teut.*
root*werz-, *wers-, *whence also* WORSE *a.*: OED)

The inchworm moth is of the family geometridae
geometer, earth measurer. The inchworm
merely moves himself and has
arranged through time his feet
into small groups, front and rear. He also
emits a thread of silk (a thread of self)
and can when so inclined divide
himself from touch to dangle
dependent upon air, to twist into
safety singly, small; like a song he rides
air and will fall again lightly.
Like light to fall upon a leaf or blade.

Why is there weight?

Couldn't even we have designed a world
of wishful movement lithely timed
minus this gravity which grinds
us into selves?

When Georgie met the great William
he was then shrinking starlike
over longish time thirty years
her senior, he wrote silken
lines, liked to land on his gathered
feet becoming cold and dense and still
credited with light which began its
journey in a brighter time. What
we do does persist, hardening
into grains, annoying into pearl.

This became his geometry: her breath
in the night next to him, both breathing
because they couldn't help it. Breathing
beneath each language, not a word
spoken without the hiss and whirr: O
there was a war, always is.

INTERVENTION IN DRAFTS

1ST DRAFT

Dear Ethan,

Get off crack.

Love,
Jessica

2ND DRAFT

Dear Ethan,

You are a selfish motherfucker.
Get off crack.

Love,
Jessica

3RD DRAFT

Dear Ethan,

Remember when I used to call you stupid
and you would cry and once you hit me
on the head with the canister vac?

I was right.

Love,
Jessica

4TH DRAFT

Dear Ethan,

This letter is only out of love
or so I've been told
You are one of only two brothers and a stepbrother
I have, and I don't want to lose you

Please get help

Love,
Jessica

5TH DRAFT

Dear Ethan,

You are not the messiah.
You are not a hip-hop artist.
You are not black because the Bible says Jews were enslaved in Egypt
and there must have been cross-pollination.

You are a crack-addicted half-Jewish half-Irish whiteboy
I can't give you money because I don't want to enable you
but please get some and buy a fucking clue

Love,
Jessica

6TH DRAFT

Dear Ethan,

The truth
is that I gave up on you years ago
I had heard enough stories
by the time you were nine and banned
from the mall for trying to return a stolen video
to the shelf
I was glad when you were caught at fourteen
breaking into cars because you left your wallet in one
(Dad talked the guy out of pressing charges—I was the one
who answered the phone)
dealing acid, selling stolen CDs, building gallon-jug bongs
out of Mom's basement (I was the one
who watched Dad tear Mom's house apart—it was the night
of the Allen Ginsberg reading)
blaming John Bailey for everything his mother blamed you for
I was glad when you were finally sent away
to Broughton
and even better to Broyhill
and even that you were caught again over your Christmas visit
and that when you came back, I was already in Ohio
I was glad when our mother forgot to tell me
about the drug dealer you fucked
who showed up at their house and pointed a gun
at our stepfather, who has never been anything but kind
(Somehow he talked the man out of killing you
Somehow he talked the man out of even waiting for you)
The supposed mugging in downtown Cleveland
that caused you to disappear
for the three days following New Year's 1999
The televisions, VCRs, camcorders your "friends" gave you
Your Wal-Mart merchandise-scanning scam

And fuck how our mother swallows your bullshit

And this
You called to tell me this
You called crying, and I even cried myself
You said you needed help, that it was all so fucked up,
and I reached out through my reservations
And you stopped talking to me
And you kept using
And I remembered to give up again

Enough. You don't deserve this much.

—Jessica

FINAL DRAFT

Our mother has asked each of us
to write you a letter
You have become your addictions
There is nothing else to say

EDWARD CURTIS'S
"A YOUNG NEZ PERCE"

Sargent would have understood you, posed
like this: wolf furs carefully unearthed from storage
and slung across an arm, a cape of glistening grays
that shower to the ground. Your upraised
fist at first looks like a woman's breast half-
exposed, so artfully do its knuckles catch
the light shimmering along the jet ridges
of your necklace quills. Below this,
long pants—shockingly voluminous—
dark as a gypsy's skirt; an ominous,
stately twist to your body that makes you appear
part politician, part dancer. So elegant an observer
with your cut-glass cheeks, you could be part
of any lady's sitting room, standing quietly alert
by the roaring fireside or the pianoforte, offering
us a glimpse of the kind of composure constituting
a character meant by birth to be observed, captured
forever by the very eyes you're meant to enrapture,
as you're all show, all gentled scandal now.
The way Virginie Gautreau
might herself have seemed, turned by the painter's
eye and hand to restive savagery: matte, black hair
and lead-white arms barely suppressed
by the dulling backdrop; flesh's glowing silhouette
snapped in by the waspish corset of a velvet gown—
Her sex, unleashed, might terrify; buckled down,
it's merely beautiful. As you are now.
Is that a human scalp hanging from your belt? We'll never know.

Some possum scrap, perhaps, a bobcat's tail, something
comfortably decorative—like the feathers trailing
from your hair. Jewelry we imagine "Mme. X" might wear,
pinned to the insipid parlor couch as her blood lips sneer
into the semblance of a smile.
Something simple, rank, and animal for us to wonder at—
to picture what it is you're holding back.

SUZY ZEUS SETS SOME LIMITS

Suzy Zeus likes guys with handguns.
Suzy Zeus likes beer in kegs.
Suzy Zeus likes breaking windows.
Suzy Zeus likes breaking eggs.
Suzy's got a boyfriend, Harry.
Touch him and she'll break your legs.

Suzy likes her sister's undies.
Suzy likes her brother Keith.
Suzy likes her father's buck knife.
Suzy likes its leather sheath.
Suzy likes her boyfriend Harry.
Touch him and she'll break your teeth.

Suzy hails from Indiana
land of crops, of Fords and farms.
Suzy lives in New York City,
land of cops and car alarms.
Suzy lives six blocks from Harry.
Touch him and she'll break your arms.

Suzy's got a kick-ass system.
Suzy is what Suzy owns.
Elton John and Cyndi Lauper,
Fleetwood Mac, the Rolling Stones
(Harry grooves to Waylon Jennings—
touch him and she'll break your bones),

Carly Simon, Sheena Easton,
Wham!, the Roches, Yes, *The Rose*,
Billy Joel, Duran Duran, and
Handel oratorios.
Harry's humming "My Sharona."
Touch him and she'll break your nose.

Suzy's got a bag of bridge mix.
Suzy's got some frozen peas.
Suzy's got a front-door dead bolt.
Harry's got a set of keys.
Harry's got a way with women.
Touch him and she'll break your knees.

Suzy stands before the mirror:
sultry, soulful, calm, complete.
Suzy loves her shapely shoulders,
likes her nose, adores her feet.
Wants a pair of mules in puce, a
pair of pumps in parakeet.

Harry asks her what she's up to.
Asks her almost every night.
Harry likes to see her naked,
see her naked in the light.
Harry never takes her dancing.
Harry says her hair's a fright.

Suzy Zeus is drinking whiskey.
Suzy Zeus is making eyes.
Suzy Zeus is making trouble
at the bar, with other guys.
Harry finds her, rips her dress off,
leaves it bunched around her thighs.

Suzy's got a can of bean dip.
Suzy's got a can of mace.
Suzy's got a Good News Bible.
Suzy's got a real nice place.
Harry's pissing out the window.
Touch him and she'll break your face.

SUZY MOVES ON

Suzy Zeus is catching fire.
Suzy Zeus is catching rays.
Suzy Nairs her legs and armpits.
Suzy fasts and Suzy prays.
Suzy wants a better boyfriend—
one who's smarter, one who stays,

one who listens, one who loves her,
one who needs her, one who knocks.
Not like Harry, banging in and
tripping on his dirty socks.
By the time he says he's sorry,
Suzy will have changed the locks.

Suzy's taking off her panties.
Suzy's taking off some weight.
Suzy's putting on mascara.
Suzy's going on a date.
Suzy knows the girl for Harry
is a girl he can inflate.

ROBIN ROBERTSON

THE PANTHER

from The Jardin Des Plantes
after Rilke

Exhausted, he sees nothing now but the bars
that flicker past him in a blur;
it seems there are a thousand bars
and behind the thousand bars an empty world.

The drill of wheel and return: turning on his heel till
he seems to pass through his own body—like whisky
swilled to the neck of the bottle then back on itself.
He swings on the pivot of his numb and baffled will.

Sometimes, though, the sprung shutter of the eyes
will slide open and let an image enter—a face, perhaps—
shooting through the tensed muscles, lightening
the limbs, streaming into his heart to die.

PATIANN ROGERS

THE LOST CREATION
OF THE EARTH

As they talked and mingled together,
the earth, the size of an orange, floated
among them through the room, slowly
turning on its axis with a not unpleasant
hum, vibrating low like the strum
of a bass string. It seemed wrapped
in silk by its clouds.

And it traveled in its orbit across
the open plains, over cornfields, keeping
pace with the train, along rushes
and scrub willows lining the creekbeds.
Cattle in the fields never raised
their heads. Following the empty
tracks at night, it was a pure white
pebble speeding through the black
against the dimmer stars.

No one on board the ship
in the thundering storm noticed
the earth dawning out of the horizon,
shining like a nugget of diamond
with sea-rain and salt. And in the spotlight
at the Cirque du Soleil, it was merely
one of nine balls circling the juggler's
head. Drums rolled. Cymbals rang.
Nothing faltered, not globes, not performer.
How its polar ice caps gleamed blue!
The audience applauded politely.

If it had been observed as itself,
it might have been seen sitting perfectly
in the hand of Christ, on the Buddha's
lap, cradled like a pearl in a shell,
cherished like a spark of mouse
in the night of a coyote's eye, rich
and wild with reverence.

The size of a crow's head, it was
that distinct against the snow as it flew
on its path, that bright through the fog,
that accurate in its courses, that brilliant
in its spheres.

ERASURE

As a Man Thinketh

serenity.

and

passion: wl

cannot distinguish them?

a philosopher on his death-be

[28]

~~compare~~ compare ~~with good will for the perfect~~
~~the~~ shadows of grief and sorrow. ~~the~~
~~confined in a~~ confined in a ~~the~~

~~pea~~

[29]

TOMAŽ ŠALAMUN

Translated by Christopher Merrill and Marko Jakše

SONNET OF A FACE

In the heart a bullet, in the bullet an ape,
in the ape a plant, in the plant a mirror.
On envelopes and in the doors—a seal.
It holds together city streets by force.
Heaven's a hoop in which the plague begins.
A field of hounds, of emperors
on horseback, of drowning deer.
But not the one I seek, brother
with one heart, one antler. A castle
veduta, a goblin and gold, the swamp
of time and my attendants.
Arrow, you slipped away from me, I'll burn
until I hit you. Dead—
my life—I'll give it back to the city.

TENEMENT

what makes pigeon
pigeon? I must know

what makes him
pick my window

wrought escape
dirty opening

keep his murmuring
from my sleep

worries his
sorry nothing nest

tethered to zero
why not fly?

pigeon! I say
I grab him round—

his feathers my fingers
catch in prayer

a shriek breaks
his hollow breast

a new sound yet
still so pigeon

so throttled
so lame

his moldy eyes
roll to the sky

nervy thing
his larded wings

leave my hands
dark as newsprint

JASON SHINDER

YOU

Stand close,
    inhale my breath.
        You're my shadow

even in the dark.
    We were born to love
        sooner or later.

We're humans.
    Aren't we?
        Don't leave

until you slip
    into the sleeves
        of my shirt.

Say something—
    and it's about
        something else

but not about us—
    which is a kind
        of loving.

For a long time
    the long falling
        of light

in the trees.
    Nothing changes.
        And the people

you've known,
     let's invite them all
        to dinner.

COVE

But I would like to talk to you when nothing has happened.
Sea of anonymous breath
                                    foiling wiretaps.
                    If you go in and out like the sea into
speaking   one soft insistence
the thread shows
shells under the limestone of monuments.
                                    Your skin brown
and lacquered with bladder wrack.
I didn't need any grand prancing but
                                    you knock yourself out.
The tide
comes in and laces a salt marsh, which
                                    doesn't want to be one or the other.
We forgot to choose sides.

You could call this sleep naive,
but we knew something.

Some say life is ugly as if the sea is not alive.
Empty out the quiet—

sweat rolls between my breasts,
the sea
        will always ignore us.

Ode upon ode hold your body in my body and there
                            rushes in quiet.
Nothing has happened, everything
has happened, inland winter with each separate needle
                            holding its drop over the ground.

THE LAKE

There is light on the geese's
hind parts tonight, my love,
birds who have some care
for their homeland, whuffing
through a lowlit sky with a hiny view on the country
left behind, yackity yacking
so loud you can probably hear them

where you are, which is far

from the smoky opiatic riches of Arabia, the hinterlands of
Afghanistan illuminated by flying shrapnel
but near to my heart which walks practically beside me

near the yellow leaves, this season's idea
of finery left on low branches, bald treetops like monks' pates;
heart leaps like the red berries hanging over the river, it's mine
for those in Taliqan who have no view of the Leonids tonight

Suspicious geese sound a sudden
alarm & all
the weekend strollers (babies in perambulators)
listen: heads up: YOU are coming home tonight
to put the ripples back in the lake

which is like saying all blackbirds will now be white
and those with "no corner of the earth distant or dark enough
to protect them" will rise under rich crimson tents, making a virtue
   of necessity so that
we shall no longer have the desire to have bodies
of substances as incorruptible as crystalline jewels:

    diamond arms, diamond legs, diamond gut
    diamond finger, diamond hair
    diamond, crystal & diamond heart
    no diamond hands, no diamond lungs
    no head made of shattering suns

INTERROGATING MR. WORM

So, this is the fool's paradise then?
The garden of metaphysical costume balls?
The thick dictionary of blank pages?
The lavender soap bubble floating off toward the infinite
From the roof of the confetti palace?

I only have faith in you, Mr. Worm.
You are bashful and yet appear unperturbed
As you go about your grim business
Underneath this hammock gilded by the setting sun
As it sways between the dark cypresses.

There's a carcass of a small animal
In the grass lush with wild flowers,
And the sound of an outdoor wedding party—
Cries and hoots as the bride spins and falls
With a white blindfold over her eyes.

MY BELOVED

after D. Khrams

In the fine print of her face
Her eyes are two loopholes.
No, let me start again.
Her eyes are flies in milk,
Her eyes are baby Draculas.

To hell with her eyes.
Let me tell you about her mouth.
Her mouth's the red cottage
Where the wolf ate Grandma.

Ah, forget about her mouth,
Let me talk about her breasts.
I get a peek at them now and then
And even that's more than enough
To make me lose my head,
So I better tell you about her legs.

When she crosses them on the sofa
It's like the jailer unwrapping a parcel
And in that parcel is a Christmas cake
And in that cake a sweet little file
That gasps her name as it files my chains.

STAND-IN

Before they strapped him in a jacket
And stuffed his mouth with a rag,
He slipped into the empty church,
Climbed the high, dim-lit cross
And clasped the suffering Jesus,

All naked himself, clinging on tight,
The fucker. Thus the pious found him,
And ran out for help, leaving him
With one candle already sputtering
Beneath his swollen, homeless feet.

DEVOTION: MEDEA

After the divorce I was a white witch fated with madness
which was a rich chemical maleness—an aroma of harm
around me like the civet of a cloudy leopard. I alarmed
myself. I was a man and a soul that loves what leaves me
hates the pleasure that's the kitchen, wants the sublime.
Who hasn't conjured up a poison dress, magnificent
in virility, a cloak of the shamans whose desires were a kiss
into submission, woman into man and disturbing distances?
I was relentless and resentful, both synonyms of the hours
I spent manufacturing mayhem to myself or spells on others
who tried to help. I didn't need help . . . I needed fuel and air.
I padded around in my bathrobe in the Very Rich Hours of my fear
and read Baudelaire and watched wrestling just for the obvious
and excruciating virtues and the beating I could see was phony,
but so was matrimony. And then it wasn't funny.
I lost the end of my nose. I looked like a sugar
skull on Diá de los Muertos. I sent the kids back to her every
   Monday—
my besneakered babies, my two betrayers—with a hat she'd forgotten
or a negligee she'd left in the laundry when she used to stay. Oh use.
Oh used to. I said sotto voce *burn to death* and then it was I
went up in flames and the others whose names I called
when they loved me were casualties of the necromancy
I cast by saying back the word *love*. Then I killed the kids with my
   sword.

LATE RETURN TO MIAMI

So many things provide a ministry.
Oven birds, for example, shade, the red hibiscus flowers
above the head of an old man asleep in Miami.
I turned all the way around and
went back the way I'd come; nothing had changed.
It's always like that someone says, always the same,
only the way we look at it varies. The world, she says,
confirming this, might be one thing only,
a permanent drive-in we circle like teenagers
in flashy cars. It's the aspects confuse us, she says,
almost whatever you want to call it, she says.

A crippled woman
goes mournfully on about her dead son, but
she can't help it. We try to forgive, but
even this is mostly grace. I drink some coffee,
wish for variance and absolution, a cheerful attitude.
It's pleasant to picture poincianas, locusts in bloom.
At noon, again at two-thirty, the
buttons on an old man's tunic shine; he hasn't moved,
or he's moved and returned.
The beautiful women sip lavender drinks.

I can't get certain beaches out of my head,
folds and configurations, a breeze revising something in the sea oats.
So many draw sustenance from their children.
It's hard to continue, we pass things around,
repeat gestures and look for a way to help.
Every well-marked path
doesn't lead somewhere. Whatever's essential,
you find someone making do without it.
Old women talking to themselves remind me of my mother;
such correspondences strike to the bone.
I turn to rivers, poems, the sun-soaked stretch
of sand beyond Fifth Street, go
up the steps, there's a wooden tower you can climb.
Up high, boys tease their girlfriends. They too stumble
around, they too return late, empty-handed.

CHARLIE SMITH

LEAVES IN THE SUBWAY

Breeze stirred by a train's
arrival lifts a green, yellow and pale red maple leaf,
spins and tosses it onto a bench where a woman in
dark blue like an old fashioned governess moves down a bit to give it
    room.

The subtlety of forgiveness is more important and the twice-told
matter of a young girl's triumph in her software class,
stays with us longer, I suppose, and then we have the carefully
placed moments in which one who has made trouble all along,
in an unfashionable flourish
and a prank conceived out of a need to quell loneliness,
attempts to catch the attention of those in the know, and fails.

I've given religion much thought and now sometimes attend services.
I don't suppose it'll hurt, unless I meet
a malefic individual who gains influence and makes me
do illegal things. But this probably won't happen. I got caught
a few years ago in an internet scam, and
spent several months
retrieving my identity, but for a while now
I've been untouched by crime. The days mount like saucers on a
    table.
I give to charity when I think of it and try not to dwell
on where the money really goes; being kind is the idea, after all.

Yesterday I drove to the mall and walked around.
The young pear trees were just transferring their business to fall.
They looked nifty and neat, not too tall and free of messy fruit.
I thought of Stendhal in his late years, still working,
without much success, and of Follain and his penetrating
sight, young girls climbing French hills
to their big or little deaths, never having
indicated much or spoken. My wife and I are planning
a move to France. It'll be fun. Next week we'll visit the embassy
to chat about expectations and services. Out my window fall's
piecing things together, sweeping up
and generally preparing the park for winter. Soon we'll be sledding
on the white Paris hills. I have a new snowsuit and boots
and can't wait to try them out. It's another way of making friends.

WASTE

Like the grain, the perfectly good
grain, spilled in the trash. And like
the copper plate, radius of rust.

Like the knives and forks which follow
their brothers. Like heirloom, cheese
cloth, cumin, oil—we lose that

which means most and least to us.
So I looked for it—the white trail
of your finish. You must have come,

pulling away, your body collapsing,
already useless. I wanted the mess
of it, the sticky dirt, the randomness,

the no-good. It was this I wanted:
your children dead in the air.

THE NICKEL WIFE

You don't hear their words
turn dull, his third glass
empty. You don't hear

Hate either, only talk
in a cove, lust talk,
the way you remember it.

A life of two circles
is circling when you show,
the nickel wife. More drink

is thus necessary
to throw the coin and still
see it, unspent, at the bottom

of all this. But the water grows
darker, the talk too, it grows
out of anything anyone says,

a cloud but no stars. You drive
her home, no—she does the long
alcohol exhale and time

evaporates, the island
rocks as never before, the seals
swim across and back,

the little bird
just not coming
to the top.

Translated by Joanna Trzeciak

LOVE AT FIRST SIGHT

They are sure
that a sudden feeling united them.
Beautiful is such certainty,
but uncertainty more beautiful.

They think, that as they didn't know each other earlier,
nothing ever happened between them.
But what would they say: those streets, stairways, and corridors
where they could have been passing each other for a long time?

I would like to ask them,
Don't you remember—
maybe face-to-face once
in a revolving door?
an "Excuse me" in a tight crowd?
a "Wrong number" heard over the phone?
—but I know their answer.
No, they don't remember.

They would be quite surprised,
that for a long time
chance had been toying with them.

Not altogether ready
to turn into their fate,
it would draw them together, pull them apart,
cut them off on their path,
and swallowing a giggle,
leap to the side.

There were signs, signals,
so what they were unreadable.
Maybe three years ago
or last Tuesday
some leaf flew
from arm to arm?
Something got lost and then got picked up.
Who knows whether it wasn't even a ball
in some childhood thicket?

There were doorknobs and doorbells,
where touch lay on touch
beforehand.
Suitcases next to one another in the baggage check.
Maybe one night the same dream,
blurred upon awakening.

Every beginning, after all,
is nothing but a sequel,
and the book of events
is always open in the middle.

Translated by Joanna Trzeciak

MIRACLE FAIR

Commonplace miracle:
that so many commonplace miracles happen.

An ordinary miracle:
in the dead of night
the barking of invisible dogs.

One miracle out of many:
a small, airy cloud
yet it can block a large and heavy moon.

Several miracles in one:
an alder tree reflected in the water,
and that it's backward left to right
and that it grows there, crown down
and never reaches the bottom,
even though the water is shallow.

An everyday miracle:
winds weak to moderate
turning gusty in storms.

First among equal miracles:
cows are cows.

Second to none:
just this orchard
from just that seed.

A miracle without a cape and top hat:
scattering white doves.

A miracle, for what else could you call it:
today the sun rose at three-fourteen
and will set at eight-oh-one.

A miracle, less surprising than it should be:
even though the hand has fewer than six fingers,
it still has more than four.

A miracle, just take a look around:
the world is everywhere.

An additional miracle, as everything is additional:
the unthinkable
is thinkable.

BONA FIDES

Cornell was a great wit and raconteur. He had an effortless
natural grace that made us feel we were all clever. He never
sought to be the center of attention, it's just that we could
never wait to see what he would say next. His wife, Priscilla,
couldn't take her eyes off of him she was so proud. He turned
out book after book, always bristling with intelligence. We all
felt so lucky to know him, to claim him as a part of our inner
circle. Without warning, he died one day. His family, about whom
we knew little, insisted that the funeral be a private affair.
We felt cheated, of course, not being able to say goodbye. He
was buried somewhere far from here. Priscilla wasn't answering
the phone. We all just wandered around in a daze, not really
wanting to get together. Cornell wasn't even cool in his grave—
wherever that was—when rumors started circulating about his affairs,
not just one or two, but perhaps dozens of them, or even hundreds.
His whole life seemed to be an intricate web of lies, and not just
to Priscilla but to all of us. Beneath the surface of the charm,
there must have been one scared, panicky animal, always planning
his next deception. I ran into Gwen downtown. "How's Priscilla
taking all of this?" I asked. "She's moved," she said. "She doesn't
want to see any of us ever again. Too painful." It all seemed
so sudden. And then the charges of plagiarism hit the papers.
The article cited endless instances of pure theft, and his life's
work was discredited, his honor lay in tatters. There seemed to be
a kind of awful joy taken in this work. His old friends in town
could barely speak of it. "Did you see that article?" "Yeah,
yeah." I never took his books down from the shelves to look at
anymore, and eventually I removed them and stored them in a box
in the garage. It wasn't long before the rumors and the articles
stopped altogether, and then it was as though he had never existed.
And, yes, Cornell had more life in him, more good cheer and warmth
and brilliance than anyone I have ever known. I had no way of

reconciling what had happened to him, what a swift, harsh vengeance had struck down his memory. I had a picture of him on the mantel, holding his glass up high, toasting the camera. We know now that he was a man of many dark secrets. Maybe his name wasn't even Cornell. Maybe he'd never gone to school. Maybe he wasn't even a human being. Maybe he was just a piece of tumbleweed that had taken on flesh for a while before blowing on, and he's laughing still. I guess no one ever knew him, but, nonetheless, we all loved him. I was getting all choked up just thinking about him and staring at the photo on the mantel when the phone rang. It was Emory. "Listen, Alex, you're not going to believe this, but I think Cornell is alive." "What?" I said. "I was in the city this weekend and I think I saw him. He's grown a mustache and dyed his hair black, but I'm sure it was him. He was eating lunch in this little Italian café with this really good-looking babe," he said. "I don't believe you, I mean, it must have been some kind of mistake, just some guy who looked a little like Cornell," I said. "It was him all right. I recognized the laugh and the gleam in his eye," he said. "Did you speak to him?" I said. "Oh no, he was no longer the Cornell that we knew. He was someone else altogether. I watched him a moment, then walked on," he said. We said good night. It didn't matter to me one way or another if he was dead or alive. Some of us had been touched by magic, and, later, people wanted to tell you it wasn't magic but a bunch of lies, you want to ask them, Who are you? Show me your bona fides. I stared at his photo until it faded from view, and there was nothing left but dust flowing across the prairie on a cold night such as this. And then I went to bed.

CRIMES OF PASSION

After Layla disappeared, Damon said she had gone to
Paris to live with her rich aunt. Layla didn't have any rich
aunt. Her whole family was as poor as church mice. Therefore,
we suspected Damon of foul play. The police just said it
happens all the time: people just disappear, especially women.
Damon said Layla was really happy in her new life. I said,
"How do you know?" He said, "She sends me letters, at least
once a week." I said, "Could I see one?" He said, "Of course
not. They're private." And that's when I decided I would
have to break into Damon's apartment. I told Flip of my plan
and he said he wanted to help. Flip went by to visit Damon,
and in the course of the conversation Damon allowed as how he
thought I might have something to do with Layla's sudden dis-
appearance. "I thought she was living in Paris with a rich
aunt," Flip said. "Layla has no rich aunt. Where did you hear
that crap? Did Jules tell you that? Because if he
did he's just trying to throw you off the track." Flip was
confused now. He'd gone there to unlock a window for me, but
now he wasn't so sure he wanted to. When Flip reported back to
me, he apologized for not carrying out his mission. He said,
"If Layla's not in Paris, what's the point of searching Damon's
apartment?" "Then why did he tell me about her letters?" I said.
"He said he suspected you, but then you'd know there couldn't
be any letters. I just don't get it," Flip said. "First of all,
why would I want to harm Layla? Layla had always been so sweet
to me," I said. "Damon is a liar, and I think he murdered
Layla because Layla was pregnant and he couldn't stand the idea of
marrying her." "Layla was pregnant?" Flip said. "Well, she
didn't exactly tell me, but that's what I've figured out since,"
I said. "Maybe she just went to one of those homes for unwed
mothers. They still exist, you know," Flip said. "Oh, Flip,
you're so naïve. Can't you see it in his eyes? He's cold-blooded.

He could do it, you know he could," I said. "It's just so hard for me to imagine anyone wanting to hurt that girl," he said. The next time I saw Damon, I said, "How is Layla doing? Are you still getting those letters?" "I think Flip's got her in his basement. He forced her to write those letters, and then he had a friend forward them to Paris. It all makes sense to me now," he said. "Flip's perfectly innocent," I said, "I would stake my life on that." "You just think you know him. Wait and see," he said. Of course I didn't believe a word he said. Flip had no motive, and he was far too innocent a man for anything like that. When we met again, I said, "How is your basement?" He said, "What?" I repeated my question, and he said, "Well, I guess it's cold and damp and dirty down there. I don't really go down there much." "Even now?" I said. "What?" he said. I repeated my question. "What are you getting at?" he said. I told him what Damon had said, and he said, "You've gotta be out of your mind. Why would I do a thing like that?" "You've always secretly loved Layla. You were jealous. You wanted her for yourself," I said. "Yes, all that's true," he said, "but that doesn't make me a kidnapper." "Well, I loved her, too," I said. We didn't mention Layla again after that. Damon and Flip and I started playing cards again on Thursday nights. I realized how fond I was of Damon. He was so bright and funny, whereas Flip seemed kind of slow. A year went by. One night when Damon and I were alone, I asked him what Layla was really like, and he said, "Who's Layla?" I said, "You've got to be kidding. Your lover, the one who disappeared." "Oh, she was just a dream, nothing more. Just something to keep us boys going on a dreary night, but she got away, and here we are."

WEREWOLF IN SELVAGE

Once, when you showed up for work
after blazing all night
someone said the trigger word
by mistake and you turned over
the things you'd stolen. Just like that.

Once, as you straightened your mask
at the Oscar bash, your friends plotted
to have you put away

Once, when you had disappeared into the woods,
you leaned over the washbasin
to have a word with me.

And when you turned back
again the roads buckled
because there was no more room in the fields,
oh loved one in the great fiery mood,
the not-asking mood.

SONG

words & sounds that build bridges toward a new tongue
within the vortex of cadences, magic weaves there
a mystery, syncopating music rising from breath of the young,

the syllables spraying forward like some cloud or mist hung
around the day, evening, under street lamps, yeasting air, where
words & sounds that build bridges toward a new tongue

gather, lace the language like fireflies stitching the night's lungs,
rhythms of new speech reinventing themselves with a flair,
a mystery, syncopating music, rising from breath of the young,

where the need for invention at the tongue's edge, high-strung,
at the edge of the cliff, becomes a risk-taking poet who shares
words & sounds that build bridges toward a new tongue,

full of wind & sun, breath feeds poetry from art's aqualungs,
under a blue sea that is sky language threads itself through air
a mystery, syncopating music, rising from breath of the young,

is a solo snatched from the throat of pure utterance, sung,
or wordsmiths bluesing cadences, weaving lines into prayers,
words & sounds that build bridges toward a new tongue—
a mystery, syncopating music, rising from breath of the young

CINDERBLOCK

On the first warm day,
the aides fret about his pate,
fetch his hat. I push him
out the automatic doors
into the pallid sun.
Dad thinks we should
stay put until all the Indians
are back in their teepees,
but right now he's off to teach
a Latin class. Where are his keys?
They're a few miles away,
in the past, where he's no longer
active in the community.
I steer him along the asphalt paths
of the grounds: bark mulch,
first green shoots,
puddle of coffee by a car.
I loop around so he can discover
the pile of construction materials twice,
the word *cinderblock* coming to him
more quickly the second time.

RECIPE: HOW TO BECOME AN IMMIGRANT AND AN EXILE

Listen. Do you hear ghosts? Connect them to the sound of a canoe
on Indian Ocean. Listen to that tape of familiar beats that has
    weathered
foreign seasons. Sukus found in Salsa. Fela Kuti meets Masekela
in Appalachia. Do not inhale the coal fumes. Hold a memory.

Commit sins of transportation. Bite the past. Spit broken teeth
and colored blood that will chart global awareness. Learn
to say fuck without flinching. Seduce anarchy of the mind and try
to order schizophrenia in realms just outside the touch of your black

hand. Image coming at you. Color it in Old English and an accented
haiku and see what you win. If lucky enough, if you are one of those
lucky cigar smoking sons of bitches, play the lottery and you might
    win
the lady's hand. Do not try to break the chains that bind her feet.

Hold her. Touch an image of her that is a mirage of you. Laugh
and say she is crazy to forget with you. Sip your beer gently.
Light up, let the sizzling seeds pass from your lips to hers. Watch
the smoke and its promise, it will turn you onto possibilities

of the night—Smile. Ghosts. As a child voices sang in my sleep
and then took to life. I dueled them with screams that were hushed
with threats of tranquility. I stole Don Quixote's sword and found
a horse in my bouncing bed and would have won the battle

but for the doctor who found malaria where there was none. Pills.
Silent duels. And so when the police with guns and big black coats
came for my father, it must have been a dream I dreamt. That
night—pills with no water but morning tea still found a newspaper

damp with dew. Swords thrust, truths as righteousness of strength
bouncing horses and Marx—it all could have been a dream. Learn
to stay up late and talk of classes and footsteps. Not of classes
but of labor at the nearest Micky D's. Dance to old rhythms

and constitute common law while talking of tradition. Find
the nearest altar. Take pills without gunpowder. Say Mandela
always with a smile. Miss her but call her a bitch. It will make
you feel like a man to stare her down feminism. Dust sprinkled

so sparsely and gently on your feet, stripped dress, gapped smile,
black hair in rainbow your laugh and the way your fingers curled
inwards—they always smelled of plums. I miss our evenings
by the pond, that time the sun refused to set and we had to roll
it over and down the hill. You never did come to say good-bye. How
is it I remember your smile at the airport? Stay away from New
York. Too many mirrors of yourself. Read Harlem only in your sleep.
Learn to say Puerto Rican radicals got what was coming to them

and Mexico is no man's land. Watch birds on National Geographic
migrate. Amuse yourself in the sound of wing against wind. Ignore

the wail of the middle passage. Find beauty in trees where no necks
were broken and burning flesh was not sacrificed and color it
    Rainbow.

You see, it's all creation. Streams, your feet washing clean. Your
    curved
elbows sending rays back to the sun. Your militant khaki skirt wet
at the folds. I sent you a letter. In it I enclosed photos of you as I will
remember you tomorrow. Sometimes I am waiting for you at our
    pond

scribbling little notes shaped like butterflies and birds that bear your
name. It's Sunday How did you leave church to come to me? I swear
you make me laugh. A hungry bird once in mid–Indian Ocean flight,
very much weakened by hunger and scared of what lay below,
    measured

wing against thigh and ate its feet. And as all must come down, it
    landed
on its head and died. My dear, eat your memories very carefully.

LET ME BE RECKLESS WITH THE WORD *LOVE*

Let me drive it into the deepest ditch
in the darkest country and pop its hood
to inspect the engine for broken valves.

Let me salvage what I can of it, hike up
my skirt and scavenge a ride from a passerby
in a pickup truck. Let him talk dirty

while chewing tobacco and listening
to Willie Nelson. When he drops me off
at your parents' house, let me walk it

through the living room, leaving tracks
in the plush pink carpet. Let it say,
I'm sorry. I seem to have made a mess.

When you shake your head, I'll blow it up
in the backyard while Doug and Donna
celebrate their anniversary. There's a word

you don't know. It means sticking with
the woman whose one foot dangles
from the window of a pickup truck.

The woman who has finally become
an apostrophe—and by that I mean not
possessive, but from Greek, *to turn away*

so you can't see her face as she detonates
the word *love* and watches it explode.

POUND, DRUNK ON A FORTY, GOES OFF

See here, what are all these birds doing
in your verse, am I to think flight or fear?
Hell I can't make heads or tails.

Sure I spent time in lockdown,
and when they let me breeze the lawn
a bunch of soap dodgers hit me up

asking what did I say on the radio
and why such nonsense in my line.
I'll show you a wad of nonsense.

Let's begin with HD—a word if I may
about that slippery one, I left her.
Not the other way around, I don't care

how many books she writes. And if a man
thinks he wants a poet of the female
variety, let him think twice.

Don't go thinking I couldn't row
the stick. O, I could row.

THE MAN WHO CONFUSES SEX WITH LOVE

Even as, at times, I may shun them,
I recognize my various proclivities.
Though my doctor says it's wrong,
I sex a corn dog, and sex a jelly doughnut;
and I sex Janis Joplin, but who doesn't?
Not that I'm incapable of refinements:
I sex that unctuous, oleaginous roll-
on-the-tongue that only the French can do,
of a *premier cru* chardonnay. Of course,
that's only "sex" in the vulgar sense,
not the real sex, as between
a man and woman, or brotherly sex,
or sex of God, sex of country.

Now love—love is another thing.
I first heard about love from a bully
down the block. When I made a sickly face,
he said, "Grow up, punk. Your parents
did it when they made you, and it's called *love*."
As for my own history, I suppose
it's not unusual for having had love
with more than I have sexed.
Not that I was into casual love—
I'm terrified of picking up a lovably
transmitted disease; nor do I buy
into the notion of sex at first sight.

So confusing, so many competing messages:
are we "making sex" or just "having love"?
Just check out, if you can stand it,

the magazines by the checkout stand:
with the "Ten Love Secrets to Drive
Your Man Crazy," or every other month
another piece on how much love
is enough: how many times a month,
or week, or day, should a couple have love.
What's the point? If you're asking me,
I'd say that love isn't anything
we should feel we have to quantify.

Still, with sex, it's hard to tell
how long it will last. You think you know
what sex is when you find it;
you can't express it enough: at first it's all
love in the bathtub, love on the sofa,
love in the wouldn't-you-like-to-know . . .
Then when you're not looking, you fall
right out of sex. Then perhaps, it comes
you meet someone, with whom sex
and the work of sex are one: the sex carries on,
doggedly, through late nights at work,
the clogged drains and the mess on the floor,
the changing of diapers, the shots;
sex gets you through the supermarket,
the doctor's office, or mowing the grass,
fixing the roof, it's all underpinned with sex,
sex planted deep inside you, long-
lived and sturdy, pulsing and firm:
it burgeons, well into your withering.

C. K. WILLIAMS

LESSONS

I.

When I offered to help her and took the arm
of the young blind woman standing
seemingly bewildered on my corner,
she thanked me, disengaged my hand
and tucked one of hers under my elbow
with a forthright, somehow heartening firmness;
we walked a few blocks to the subway
and rode awhile in the same direction;
she studied history, she told me, then here
was my stop, that's all there was time for.

2.

Something about feeling the world
come towards her in irrational jags,
a hundred voices a minute, honks,
squeals, the clicking blur of a bike,
and how she let herself flow across it
with the most valiant, unflinching unsurprise
made the way I dwell in my own cognition,
the junctures of perception and thought,
seem suddenly hectic, blunt,
the sense of abundances squandered, misused.

3.

My first piano teacher was partly blind;
her sister, whom she lived with,
was entirely so: she had a guide dog,
a shepherd, who'd snarl at me from their yard—
I feared him nearly as much as my teacher.
She, of the old school, cool and severe,
because of her sight would seem to *glare* at my fingers,

and she kept a baton on the keyboard to rap them
for their inexhaustible store of wrong notes
and for lags of my always inadequate attention.

4.

Still, to bring her back just to berate her
is unfair, I mustn't have been easy either.
I keep being drawn to that place, though:
there was some scent there, some perfume, some powder;
my ears would ring and my eyes widen and tear.
Rank, wild, it may have been perspiration—
they were poor—or old music, or books;
two women, a dog: despite myself,
stumbling out into the dusk—dear dusk—
I'd find myself trying to breathe it again.

5.

. . . And the way one can find oneself strewn
so inattentively across life, across time.
Those who touch us, those whom we touch,
we hold them or we let them go
as though it were such a small matter.
How even know in truth how much
of mind should be memory, no less
what portion of self should be others
rather than self? Across life, across time,
as though it were such a small matter.

C. K. WILLIAMS

SCALE

SCALE: I

Catherine shrieks
a little then comes
over to show me
where something bit her.

Stationing herself
flank to my face
she jerks her shirt
out of her jeans—

the smallest segment
of skin, so smooth,
though, so densely
resilient, so *present*,

that the whole inside
of my body goes
achingly hollow,
and floods with lust.

———

No sign of a sting;
Catherine tucks
herself in and goes
back to her work-

bench to hammer

again at the links
she's forging
for a necklace,

leaving me to act
as though nothing
had changed,
as though this moment

I'm caught in
could go on expanding
like this forever,
with nothing changed.

SCALE: II

Once, hearing you behind me, I turned,
you were naked, I hadn't known you would be,

and something in my sense of dimension went awry,
so your body, the volumes of your shoulders and hips,

the broad expanse of your chest over your breasts
and the long, sleek slide down between

seemed all at once larger, more than that, vast:
you were lavish, daunting, a deluge of presence.

I wanted to touch you, but I looked away;
it wasn't desire I felt, or not only desire,

I just didn't want ordinary existence to resume,
as though with you there could be such a thing.

TENDER

A tall-masted white sailboat works laboriously across a wave-tossed
   bay;
when it tilts in the swell, a porthole reflects a dot of light that darts
   towards me,
skitters back to refuge in the boat, gleams out again, and timidly
   retreats,
like a thought that comes almost to mind but slips away into the
   general glare.

An inflatable tender, tethered to the stern, just skims the commotion
   of the wake:
within it will be oars, a miniature motor, and, tucked into a pocket,
   life vests.
Such reassuring redundancy: don't we desire just such an accessory,
   faith perhaps,
or at a certain age to be comforted, not daunted, by knowing one will
   really die?

To bring all that with you, by compulsion admittedly, but on such a
   slender leash,
and so maneuverable it is, tractable, so nearly frictionless, no need to
   strain;
though it might have to rush a little to keep up, you hardly know it's
   there:
that insouciant headlong scurry, that always ardent leaping forward
   into place.

THE WEDDING OF IGNATZ

Weight
is the end

of wanting.

The simples
gleaming

in their rests.

———

In the game called
hypothesis

an orange

is gripped between the chin
and shoulder

then is transferred

to the chin
and shoulder of

the next-in-line. Then

a flaming log
is rolled

into the river. Then

a chalk circle
is drawn

around each plate.

— — —

One day I walked
to the window

robed in the loveliest
robe of the year.

One day I knelt down
by the fountain.

A crown of parsley
a crown of dill.

One day my hands
closed on the handles.

A match tip was placed
beneath my tongue.

— — —

"Listen to me—someone
has tricked you.

There never was an apple."

SELF SEARCH

When we look around for proof
of basic epistemological matters,
that life isn't only seemings smattered,
a dream brought on by snaggled meat,
often the self blocks the view
of the tree or cat or car race
so all we find are me-leaves, me-meows,
me-machines of speedy impulse-me.
Maybe the point's to see the self
as a kind of film that tints everything
bluer, more youer, and yet look through,
whatever you have to do, volunteer
at a shelter changing the abandoned
hamster's litter, put together a coat drive
for the poor, go door-to-door for your candidate,
be devoted to a lover or lose yourself
cheering in a crowd, Go Hens! Go
higher, go lower, to see perhaps the sky
as a rock might, meditate until you become
a beam of light, be divided as a 3 by 27
and not get overcome by your identity ending
or expect to reappear after the decimal.
Perhaps we should be practicing not having
a self to claim, one day it's baggage
we're without, no longer waiting
for it to squirt out onto the conveyor belt
with all the others that look so much alike.
Yet it's sad to imagine no me around
to press his nose into your sleeping hair.
I worry death won't care, just a bunch of dust
rushing up, some addled flashes, chills
then nill. I like too much that old idea

of heaven, everyone and pet you've lost
comes running up which could not happen
if there's no me there to meet.
Self, I'm stuck with you
but the notion of becoming unglued is too much
and brings tears that come, of course,
because you're such a schmuck. Some days
you crash about raving how ignored you are
then why the hell don't people let you alone
but I've seen you too perform small
nobilities, selfless generosities.
One way or the other, we'll party I'm sure
and you'll take me with you?

Translated by Clare Cavanagh

LITTLE WALTZ

The days are so vivid, so bright
that even the slim, sparse palms
are covered in the white dust of neglect.
Serpents in the vineyards slither softly,
but the evening sea grows dark and,
suspended overhead like punctuation
in the highest script, the seagulls barely stir.
A drop of wine's inscribed upon your lips.
The limestone hills slowly melt
on the horizon and a star appears.
At night on the square an orchestra of sailors
dressed in spotless white
plays a little waltz by Shostakovich; small children
cry as if they'd guessed
what the merry music's really saying.
We've been locked in the world's box,
love sets us free, time kills us.

MAKING BUTTER

(video transcript of three people in their twenties making butter on March 16, 2002)

Is this too much?
I think it might be easier to shake if you don't have too much.
We're going to give a little bit to Eric here.
Now we're going to make some butter.
We're going to start shaking it.
Do we have any faster music?
We need faster music, faster music.
This is a workout.
I don't feel anything anymore.
Now, no it's not done yet.
It's whipped cream.
Don't do that.
Wait, we can put on faster music.
It's getting heavy.
Oh I got the trick now.
This feels really obscene.
Zero to nothing.
I'm starting to feel it.
Should we test it?
Oh my god.
Almost butter.
Oh my god.
It works.
It's not butter yet.
It's still whipped cream.
Is it butter yet?
This is getting in the way.
There is water leaking out.
It hardened and the liquid is coming out.

Now it's getting into a solid.
I need a plastic bag.
It's like a solid that is flipping up and down.
Oh my god, weird.
Wow.
This is what it actually.
Oh my god.
We made butter.
Mine is really slippery.
You have to have this milky stuff.
We made butter.

CONTRIBUTORS

AGHA SHAHID ALI (1949–2001) grew up Muslim in Kashmir and was educated at the University of Kashmir, Srinagar, and the University of Delhi. His volumes of poetry include *Call Me Ishmael Tonight: A Book of Ghazals* (2003); *Rooms Are Never Finished* (2001); *The Country Without a Post Office* (1997); *The Beloved Witness: Selected Poems* (1992); *A Nostalgist's Map of America* (1991); *A Walk Through the Yellow Pages* (1987); *The Half-Inch Himalayas* (1987); *In Memory of Begum Akhtar and Other Poems* (1979); and *Bone Sculpture* (1972). Ali received fellowships from the Pennsylvania Council on the Arts, the Bread Loaf Writers' Conference, the Ingram-Merrill Foundation, the New York Foundation for the Arts, and the Guggenheim Foundation and was awarded a Pushcart Prize. He held teaching positions at the University of Delhi, Penn State, SUNY Binghamton, Princeton University, Hamilton College, Baruch College, the University of Utah, and Warren Wilson College.

YEHUDA AMICHAI (1924–2000) emigrated to Jerusalem with his parents at the age of twelve and became one of the first poets to write in colloquial Hebrew, authoring fourteen books and winning the Israel Prize in 1982. He is considered one of the great poets of the twentieth century. The recipient of numerous awards, his work has been translated into more than thirty-seven languages.

STEPHANIE ANDERSON's work has appeared in *American Letters & Commentary*, *Boston Review*, *Denver Quarterly*, and *Octopus*, among other publications. She is the author of *In the Particular Particular*, winner of the 2006 DIAGRAM/New Michigan Press Chapbook Prize. She currently lives and studies in Chicago.

RAE ARMANTROUT's most recent book of poetry, *Next Life* (2007), was chosen as one of the 100 Notable Books of 2007 by the *New York Times*. Other recent books include *Collected Prose* (2007); *Up to Speed*

(2004); *The Pretext* (2001); and *Veil: New and Selected Poems* (2001). Her poems have been included in anthologies such as *Postmodern American Poetry: A Norton Anthology* (1993); *American Women Poets in the 21st Century: Where Language Meets the Lyric Tradition* (2002); *The Oxford Book of American Poetry* (2006); and *The Best American Poetry* of 1988, 2001, 2002, 2004, and 2007. Armantrout received an award in poetry from the Foundation for Contemporary Arts in 2007 and a Guggenheim Fellowship in 2008. She is Professor of Poetry and Poetics at the University of California, San Diego.

REBECCA ARONSON's poems have appeared in *Ecotone*, the *Georgia Review*, and *Quarterly West*, among other publications; her first book is *Creature, Creature* (Main-Traveled Roads Press, 2007). She lives in Albuquerque, New Mexico, where she teaches poetry and serves as a contributing editor for the *Laurel Review*.

WILLIS BARNSTONE's publications include *Modern European Poetry* (1967); *The Other Bible* (1984); *The Secret Reader: 501 Sonnets* (1996); the memoir biography *With Borges on an Ordinary Evening in Buenos Aires* (1993); and *To Touch the Sky* (1999). His literary translation of the New Testament, *The New Covenant: The Four Gospels and Apocalypse*, was published by Riverhead Books in 2002.

The late AMY BARTLETT was the founding poetry editor of *Tin House* magazine.

ERIN BELIEU is the author of two collections of poetry. The first, *Infanta* (Copper Canyon Press, 1995), was selected by Hayden Carruth for the National Poetry Series and was named one of the ten best books of 1995 by *Library Journal*, the National Book Critics Circle, and the *Washington Post Book World*. Her second collection, *One Above and One Below* (Copper Canyon Press, 2000), won the Ohioana Award and the Society of Midland Authors Award.

MOLLY BENDALL is the author of three books of poems, most recently *Ariadne's Island*.

JILL BIALOSKY is the author of three poetry collections, *The End of Desire* (1997); *Subterranean* (2001), a finalist for the James Laughlin Prize from the Academy of American Poets; and *Intruder* (2008). She is also the author of two novels, *House Under Snow* (2002) and, most recently, *The Life Room* (2007). She coedited with Helen Schulman *Wanting a Child* (1998). Bialosky's poems and essays have been published in many magazines, including the *New Yorker*, the *Nation*, the *Atlantic Monthly*, *Redbook*, *O Magazine*, *Kenyon Review*, *Antioch Review*, the *New Republic*, *Paris Review*, *Poetry*, *American Poetry Review*, and *TriQuarterly*. Bialosky is an editor at W. W. Norton & Company and lives in New York City.

MARK BIBBINS is the author of two collections of poems, *The Dance of No Hard Feelings* (Copper Canyon, 2009) and the Lambda Award-winning *Sky Lounge*. He lives in New York City and teaches at the New School.

FRANK BIDART's most recent full-length collections of poetry are *Star Dust* (FSG, 2005); *Desire* (FSG, 1997); and *In the Western Night: Collected Poems 1965–90* (FSG, 1990). He has won many prizes, including the 2007 Bollingen Prize in American Poetry. *Watching the Spring Festival*, Bidart's first collection of lyric poems, will be published by FSG in April 2008.

THORDIS BJORNSDOTTIR is an award-winning Icelandic poet and novelist who has published several books in Icelandic, beginning in 2004. One of these, *Vera & Linus* (2006), is available in English. She is working now on translating a collection of poetry and also her latest novel, *Saga af Bláu Sumri* (*A Tale of a Blue Summer*).

CHANA BLOCH is a poet, translator, and literary critic. She is the author of three books of poems, *The Secrets of the Tribe*, *The Past Keeps Changing*, and *Mrs. Dumpty*. She is cotranslator of the biblical *Song of Songs* as well as four books of contemporary Israeli poetry: *The Selected Poetry* and *Open Closed Open,* by Yehuda Amichai, and *A Dress of Fire* and *The Window*, by Dahlia Ravikovitch. Among her awards are two fellowships from the National Endowment for the Arts, in poetry and in translation; a fellowship from the National Endowment for the Humanities;

the Writers Exchange Award of Poets & Writers; two Pushcart Prizes; and the Discovery Award of the 92nd Street Y Poetry Center.

JOEL BROUWER is the author of the poetry collections *Exactly What Happened*, *Centuries*, and *And So*.

WENDY BURK is a poet and translator. She has twice been named artist-in-residence with the National Park Service (2001, Isle Royale National Park; 2003, Buffalo National River).

ERIK CAMPBELL has recently returned to the States after five years in Papua, Indonesia, where he worked as a technical writer for an American mining company. His poems and essays have appeared or are forthcoming in the *Iowa Review*, the *Massachusetts Review*, the *Southern Poetry Review*, and other literary journals. He has been nominated twice for a Pushcart Prize in poetry, and his first poetry collection, *Arguments for Stillness* (2006), was named by Book Sense as one of the top ten poetry collections for 2007.

CLARE CAVANAGH has translated numerous volumes of Polish poetry and prose, most notably the work of Adam Zagajewski and Wislawa Szymborska. She is the author of *Osip Mandelstam and the Modernist Creation of Tradition* (1995) and *Poetry and Power: Russia, Poland and the West*, forthcoming from Yale University Press. She is currently working on an authorized biography of Czeslaw Milosz, entitled *Czeslaw Milosz and His Century: A Critical Life*, which will be published by Farrar, Straus, and Giroux.

LYNN AARTI CHANDHOK's first book, *The View from Zero Bridge* (2007), won the 2006 Philip Levine Prize. She received a 2008 Glenna Luschei Prize from *Prairie Schooner*, as well as the 2006 Morton Marr Poetry Prize from *Southwest Review*. Her work has appeared in the *New Republic*, the *Antioch Review*, the *Hudson Review*, the *Missouri Review*, and *Sewanee Theological Review*, on *Poetry Daily*, and in the anthology *Poetry Daily Essentials 2007*. She teaches high school English in Brooklyn, New York, where she lives with her husband and two daughters.

VICTORIA CHANG's second book of poems will be published in 2008 by the University of Georgia Press, as part of the VQR Poetry Series. Her first book won the *Crab Orchard Review* Open Competition Prize in Poetry and was published by Southern Illinois University Press in 2005. It won the Association of Asian American Studies Book Award. Her poetry has appeared in or is forthcoming in publications such as the *Paris Review, Poetry,* the *New Republic,* the *Nation, Slate, New England Review,* the *Washington Post, Triquarterly, Ploughshares, Threepenny Review, Kenyon Review,* and *The Best American Poetry 2005.* She also edited an anthology titled *Asian American Poetry: The Next Generation,* published by the University of Illinois Press (2004).

BILLY COLLINS is the author of eight collections of poetry: his latest is *Ballistics* (Random House, 2008). He is a Distinguished Professor of English at Lehman College (CUNY) and a former United States poet laureate (2001–03).

Zhao Zhenkai was born on August 2, 1949, in Beijing. His pseudonym, BEI DAO, literally means "North Island" and was suggested by a friend as a reference to the poet's provenance from Northern China as well as his typical solitude. Dao was exiled from China after the Tiananmen Square massacre of 1989. His books of poetry include *Unlock* (2000); *At the Sky's Edge: Poems 1991–1996* (1996); *Landscape Over Zero* (1995); *Forms of Distance* (1994); *Old Snow* (1991); and *The August Sleepwalker* (1990). His work has been translated into over twenty-five languages. His awards and honors include the Aragana Poetry Prize from the International Festival of Poetry in Casablanca, Morocco, and a Guggenheim Fellowship. In 2006, Bei Dao was allowed to move back to China.

OLENA KALYTIAK DAVIS is the author of two collections of poetry, *shattered sonnets love cards and other off and back handed importunites* (2003), a Spring 2004 Book Sense Poetry Top Ten Pick, and *And Her Soul Out Of Nothing* (1997), which was selected by Rita Dove for the Brittingham Prize in Poetry. Her poems have appeared in numerous journals and anthologies, including four *The Best American Poetry* volumes, and have won a Pushcart Prize. The recipient of a Guggenheim Fellowship, a Rona Jaffe Foundation writers grant, several grants from the Alaska and Juneau Arts Councils, and, most recently, a fellowship from the Rasmuson Foundation, she writes and raises her two children in Anchorage, Alaska.

ALEŠ DEBELJAK, a poet, cultural critic, and translator, has won several awards, including the Slovenian National Book Award, the Miriam Lindberg Israel Poetry for Peace Prize, and the Chiqu Poetry Prize. His books have appeared in English, Japanese, German, Croatian, Macedonian, Serbian, Polish, Hungarian, Czech, Slovak, Lithuanian, Finnish, French, Italian, Spanish, and Romanian translations. His recent publications in English include three books of poems, *Anxious Moments*, *The City and the Child*, and *Dictionary of Silence*. He is the general editor of the book series Terra Incognita: Writings from Central Europe, published by White Pine Press.

MÓNICA DE LA TORRE is the author of the poetry books *Talk Shows* (2007) and *Acúfenos*, published in 2006 in Mexico City by Taller Ditoria. She is coauthor of the artist book *Appendices, Illustrations & Notes*, available on Ubu.com and coedited the multilingual anthology *Reversible Monuments: Contemporary Mexican Poetry* with Michael Wiegers (Copper Canyon Press). She is senior editor at *BOMB Magazine* and lives in Brooklyn. *Public Domain*, her most recent poetry collection, has just been released by Roof Books.

DARCIE DENNIGAN's first book of poems, *Corinna A-Maying the Apocalypse*, was chosen by Alice Fulton for the 2007 Poets Out Loud Prize. Her poems and nonfiction have appeared in the *Atlantic Monthly*, *The Believer*, *Forklift Ohio*, *jubilat*, and elsewhere and anthologized in *180 More: Extraordinary Poems for Every Day*. She is the recipient of a Discovery/*The Nation* award and fellowships from the Bread Loaf Writers' Conference and the Byrdcliffe Artists' Guild. She lives in Rhode Island.

ROB DENNIS's work has appeared in the *Paris Review*, *Fence*, and the *Electronic Poetry Review*. He lives in New York City and works for a hedge fund in Connecticut.

MATTHEW DICKMAN is the author of *All-American Poem*, the 2008 APR/Honickman First Book Prize published through Copper Canyon Press. His work has appeared in the *Boston Review*, *Narrative*, *American Poetry Review*, and the *New Yorker*, among other publications. He lives in Portland, Oregon.

MICHAEL DICKMAN lives in Portland, Oregon. His work has appeared in the *American Poetry Review*, *Field*, and the *New Yorker*. Copper Canyon Press will publish his first book, *The End of the West*, next spring.

BEN DOLLER (né Doyle)'s first book of poems, *Radio, Radio*, was selected by Susan Howe as winner of the 2000 Walt Whitman Award. His second book, *FAQ:*, will be published by Ahsahta Press in 2009, and his third book, *Dead Ahead*, is forthcoming from Fence Books. He coedits the Kuhl House Contemporary Poets series and teaches in Antioch's low-res MFA program. Wherever he lives, he lives with his lady, Sandra Doller (née Miller), and their boxador, Ronald Johnson.

MARK DOTY's eighth book of poems, *Fire To Fire: New and Selected Poems*, appeared from HarperCollins in 2008. He's also published four volumes of nonfiction prose; the most recent, *Dog Years*, was a *New York Times* best-seller and has recently been published in Brasil, Italy, France, and the United Kingdom. In the fall of 2009, he'll join the faculty at Rutgers. He lives in New York City.

CAROL ANN DUFFY is the author of *Standing Female Nude* (1985), winner of a Scottish Arts Council Award; *Selling Manhattan* (1987), which won a Somerset Maugham Award; *The Other Country* (1990); *Mean Time* (1993), which won the Whitbread Poetry Award and the Forward Poetry Prize (Best Poetry Collection of the Year); *The World's Wife* (1999); *Feminine Gospels* (2002); and *Rapture* (2005), winner of the 2005 T. S. Eliot Prize. She received an Eric Gregory Award in 1984 and a Cholmondeley Award in 1992 from the Society of Authors, the Dylan Thomas Award from the Poetry Society in 1989, and a Lannan Literary Award from the Lannan Foundation (USA) in 1995. She was awarded an OBE in 1995 and a CBE in 2001 and became a Fellow of the Royal Society of Literature in 1999.

STEPHEN DUNN is the author of fifteen collections of poems, including *Different Hours*, which won the Pulitzer Prize. A new collection of selected and new poems from 1995 to 2009, entitled *What Goes On*, will be issued by Norton in early 2009. He lives in Frostburg, Maryland.

THOMAS SAYERS ELLIS's first full collection, *The Maverick Room*, was published by Graywolf Press in 2005, for which he received a Mrs. Giles Whiting Writers' Award and the 2006 John C. Zacharis First Book Award. He is also the author of *The Good Junk* (1996); the chapbook *The Genuine Negro Hero* (2001); and the chaplet *Song On* (2005). His *Breakfast and Blackfist: Notes for Black Poets* is forthcoming from the University of Michigan Press, Poets on Poetry Series. His work has appeared in many journals and anthologies, including *Poetry*, *Grand Street*, *Ploughshares*, and *The Best American Poetry* 1997 and 2001. He has received fellowships and grants from the Fine Arts Work Center, the Ohio Arts Council, Yaddo, and the MacDowell Colony.

ELAINE EQUI's latest book, *Ripple Effect: New & Selected Poems*, was a finalist for the *L.A. Times* Book Award and on the short list for the Griffin Poetry Prize. She has published many other collections of poetry, including *Surface Tension*, *Decoy*, and *Voice-Over*, which won the San Francisco State Poetry Award. Her work is widely anthologized and appears in *Postmodern American Poetry: A Norton Anthology* and in several editions of *The Best American Poetry*. She teaches at New York University and in the MFA programs at the New School and City College.

GIBSON FAY-LEBLANC's poems have appeared in magazines including *Guernica*, the *New Republic*, *Prairie Schooner*, *Poetry Northwest*, and *Verse Daily*. He has taught writing at Columbia, Fordham, and the University of Southern Maine, as well as in secondary schools across the country, and currently directs the Telling Room, a nonprofit community writing center in Portland, Maine.

MONICA FERRELL's poems have appeared in the *New York Review of Books*, *Fence*, *Paris Review*, and other magazines. A former Discovery/*The Nation* winner and Wallace Stegner Fellow at Stanford University, she is also the author of a novel, *The Answer is Always Yes*, forthcoming from

Random House in April 2008. Her first poetry collection, *Beasts for the Chase*, won the 2007 Kathryn A. Morton Prize in Poetry.

ZACK FINCH is a PhD candidate in poetics at SUNY Buffalo. His poems have appeared in various journals, such as *Radical Society*, *Poetry*, and *American Letters & Commentary*. He teaches periodically in the creative writing program at Dartmouth College.

NICK FLYNN's *Another Bullshit Night in Suck City* (2004) won the PEN/ Martha Albrand Award, was shortlisted for France's Prix Femina, and has been translated into thirteen languages. He is also the author of two books of poetry, *Some Ether* (2000) and *Blind Huber* (2002), for which he received fellowships from, among other organizations, the Guggenheim Foundation and the Library of Congress. Some of the venues his poems, essays, and nonfiction have appeared in include the *New Yorker*, the *Paris Review*, National Public Radio's *This American Life*, and the *New York Times Book Review*.

HELEN RUTH FREEMAN (1917–2007) was the author of several volumes of poetry, including *Diurnal Matters*, *A Certain Distance*, *The Fugitive Season*, and *The Far Field*. She was a founding member of the board of directors of Poets House.

TIFFANY NOELLE FUNG hails from Portland, Oregon, and received an MFA from Columbia University. Her poems have appeared in *Tin House*, nycbigcitylit.com, indigestmag.com, among others. She is the former managing editor of GuernicaMag.com and currently lives and works in New York City.

JAMES GALVIN's seventh book of poems is due out from Copper Canyon Press this coming spring. He also has two prose books published by Henry Holt. He is the recipient of grants from the Lannan Foundation, the Lila Wallace-Readers Digest Foundation, the Ingram Merrill Foundation, the Guggenheim Foundation, and the National Endowment for the Arts. When he isn't in Wyoming, where he has some land and some horses, he teaches at the Iowa Writers' Workshop.

PETER GIZZI is the author of *The Outernationale, Some Values of Landscape and Weather, Artificial Heart*, and *Periplum and Other Poems 1987–1992*. He has also published several limited-edition chapbooks, folios, and artist books. His work has been translated into numerous languages and anthologized here and abroad. His honors include the Lavan Younger Poet Award from the Academy of American Poets and fellowships in poetry from the Fund for Poetry, the Rex Foundation, the Howard Foundation, the Foundation for Contemporary Arts, and the John Simon Guggenheim Memorial Foundation. He has held residencies at the MacDowell Colony, the Foundation of French Literature at Royaumont, Un Bureau Sur L'Atlantique, and the Centre International de Poesie Marseille (cipM). His editing projects have included *o·blēk: a journal of language arts, The Exact Change Yearbook, The House That Jack Built: The Collected Lectures of Jack Spicer*, and *My Vocabulary Did This to Me: The Collected Poetry of Jack Spicer*. He is currently the poetry editor for the *Nation*. He works at the University of Massachusetts, Amherst.

DONALD HALL was poet laureate of the United States 2006–07. He has published twenty books of poetry, most recently a collection of new and selected poems titled *White Apples and the Taste of Stone* (2006). In September of 2008, on his eightieth birthday, he published a memoir called *Unpacking the Boxes*. He was born in Connecticut and since 1975 has lived in a family farmhouse in New Hampshire, for twenty years with his wife, Jane Kenyon (1947–1995).

HEATHER HARTLEY is Paris editor for *Tin House* magazine and her poetry manuscript *Knock Knock* was a finalist in the 2007 National Poetry Series and a finalist for the 2008 Dorset Tupelo Prize. Her poems have appeared in *Post Road*, the *Los Angeles Review, Mississippi Review, POOL, Saint Petersburg Review, Forklift Ohio*, and elsewhere. Her essays, interviews, and short pieces have appeared in the 2007 *Best American Nonrequired Reading, Food & Booze: A Tin House Literary Feast*, and *The World Within: Writers Talk Ambition, Angst, Anarchy . . .*

MATTHEA HARVEY is the author of three books of poetry: *Modern Life* (2007), a finalist for the National Book Critics Circle Award; *Sad Little Breathing Machine* (2004); and *Pity the Bathtub Its Forced Embrace of the*

Human Form (2000). She is a contributing editor to *jubilat*, *BOMB*, and *Meatpaper*. She teaches poetry at Sarah Lawrence and lives in Brooklyn. Her Web site is http://www.mattheaharvey.info.

CHRISTIAN HAWKEY is the author of three books of poetry: *The Book of Funnels*, *HourHour*, and *Citizen Of*.

TERRANCE HAYES is the author of *Wind in a Box* (2006); *Hip Logic* (2002); and *Muscular Music* (Carnegie Mellon University Contemporary Classics, 2005 and Tia Chucha Press, 1999). His honors include a Whiting Writers Award, the Kate Tufts Discovery Award, a National Poetry Series Award, a Pushcart Prize, two *The Best American Poetry* selections, and a National Endowment for the Arts Fellowship. His poems have appeared in a range of journals, including the *New Yorker*, the *Kenyon Review*, and *Ploughshares*. He is a professor of creative writing at Carnegie Mellon University and lives in Pittsburgh, Pennsylvania, with his family.

SEAMUS HEANEY has published hundreds of poems in such collections as *District and Circle* (2006); *Opened Ground* (1999), which was named a *New York Times* Notable Book of the Year; *The Spirit Level* (1996); *Selected Poems 1966–1987* (1990); and *Sweeney Astray* (1984). He is also cotranslator, with Stanislaw Baranczak, of *Laments: Poems of Jan Kochanowski* (1995) and coauthor, with Joseph Brodsky and Derek Walcott, of a collection of essays entitled *Homage to Robert Frost* (1996). Heaney is a Foreign Member of the American Academy of Arts and Letters and held the chair of Professor of Poetry at Oxford from 1989 to 1994. In 1995 he received the Nobel Prize in Literature.

JANE HIRSHFIELD's books of poetry include *After* (2006); *Given Sugar, Given Salt* (2001), which was a finalist for the National Book Critics Circle Award; *The Lives of the Heart* (1997); *The October Palace* (1994); *Of Gravity & Angels* (1988); and *Alaya* (1982). She is the author of *Nine Gates: Entering the Mind of Poetry* (1997) and has also edited and translated *The Ink Dark Moon: Poems by Ono no Komachi and Izumi Shikibu, Women of the Ancient Court of Japan* (1990) with Mariko Aratani and *Women in Praise of the Sacred: Forty-Three Centuries of Spiritual Poetry by Women* (1994). Her honors include the Poetry Center Book Award, fellowships from the Guggenheim and Rockefeller foundations, Columbia University's Translation Center Award, the Commonwealth Club of California Poetry Medal, and the Bay Area Book Reviewers Award. In 2004, Hirshfield was awarded the 70th Academy Fellowship for distinguished poetic achievement by the Academy of American Poets.

SIR MUHAMMAD IQBAL (1877–1938) was a Muslim poet, philosopher, and politician born in Sialkot, British India (now in Pakistan), whose poetry in Urdu and Persian is considered to be among the greatest of the modern era and whose vision of an independent state for the Muslims of British India inspired the creation of Pakistan.

MARKO JAKŠE, born 1959, is one of the most controversial and interesting contemporary Slovenian painters. He worked on Tomaž Šalamun's poems while he lived in New York.

RAFIQ KATHWARI is a multilingual freelance reporter and photographer. Kathwari's poetry has been featured in the *Literary Review* and on National Public Radio and anthologized in *Ravishing Disunities: Real Ghazals in English* (Wesleyan University, 1999).

Some of PETER KLINE's recent work has appeared in *Poetry*, *Best New Poets 2006*, *Poet Lore*, *Meridian*, *Cold Mountain*, the *Mississippi Review*, and *Poetry Miscellany*. He is currently a Wallace Stegner Fellow at Stanford University.

CHANA KRONFELD is the author of *On the Margins of Modernism* (1995), which won the MLA Scaglione Prize in 1998 for Best Book in Comparative Literary Studies. Her cotranslation (with Chana Bloch) of Yehuda Amichai's *Open Closed Open* (2002) won the National Endowment for the Arts and the Marie Syrkin awards. In 2005–06 Kronfeld and Bloch received the top NEA award for their translation of *The Poetry of Dahlia Ravikovitch*, forthcoming from W. W. Norton.

BRETT FLETCHER LAUER's poems have appeared in *Boston Review*, *Denver Quarterly*, *Pleiades*, and *Slope*.

KRISTA J. H. LEAHY is a writer living in Brooklyn. Her poetry has appeared in *Free Lunch*, *Indefinite Space*, and *Podium*.

KELLY LE FAVE's poems have appeared in *Image*, the *Notre Dame Review*, *Painted Bride Quarterly*, the *Massachusetts Review*, and other journals. Her book manuscript *Me Comma You* won the 2002 Gibbs-Smith Poetry Prize and was published by Gibbs Smith. Le Fave is a founding editor of the internationally distributed literary journal *jubilat*. She has taught writing at Syracuse University; the University of Massachusetts, Amherst; and the University of Utah.

DAVID LEHMAN is the author of several collections of poems, including *When a Woman Loves a Man* (2005); *Jim and Dave Defeat the Masked Man* (with James Cummins, 2005); *The Evening Sun* (2002); *The Daily Mirror: A Journal in Poetry* (2000); *Valentine Place* (1996); *Operation Memory* (1990); and *An Alternative to Speech* (1986). He is series editor of *The Best American Poetry*, which he initiated in 1988, and is general editor of the University of Michigan Press's Poets on Poetry Series. Recently, Lehman edited *The Oxford Book of American Poetry* (2006). His honors include fellowships from the Guggenheim Foundation, the Ingram Merrill Foundation, and the National Endowment for the Arts; an award in literature from the American Academy of Arts and Letters; and a Lila Wallace-Reader's Digest Writer's Award.

ALEX LEMON's poetry collections include *Hallelujah Blackout* (2007) and *Mosquito* (2006). A memoir is also forthcoming from Scribner. Among his awards are a 2005 Literature Fellowship in Poetry from the National Endowment for the Arts and a 2006 Minnesota Arts Board Grant. He coedits *LUNA: A Journal of Poetry and Translation* with Ray Gonzalez and is a frequent contributor to the *Bloomsbury Review*. He teaches at TCU in Fort Worth, Texas.

Although BEI LING was not at Tiananmen Square in the spring of 1989 during the pro-democracy protests, he was censured in absentia by the Chinese government for his calls for democratic reform. While at Harvard in the mid-1990s, Ling founded *Tendency*, a literary journal and press of dissidents and writers-in-exile in the Chinese language.

He also founded the Independent Chinese PEN Center. In 1999, Ling returned to China and on August 11, 2000, he and his brother were arrested in Beijing for illegally printing and publishing *Tendency*. The arrests prompted immediate international protests. Ling and his brother were released on August 25, 2000.

TIMOTHY LIU has two new books forthcoming, *Bending the Mind around the Dream's Blown Fuse* (Talisman House) and *Polytheogamy* (Saturnalia Books). He lives in Manhattan.

FEDERICO GARCÍA LORCA (1898–1936) is one of Spain's greatest and most influential poets. He wrote plays, including the classic *The House of Bernarda Alba* and *Blood Wedding*, numerous essays, and approximately 1,120 pages of poetry. His *Poet in New York* is considered a defining work of modern literature.

A. LOUDERMILK's *The Daughterliest Son* won the Swan Scythe Press 2001 Chapbook Contest. The full-length manuscript *Daring Love* was a finalist in 2001 for both Tupelo Press and Sarabande Books poetry contests. Poems appear in the *Mississippi Review*, the *Madison Review*, the *Redneck Review*, *Rhino*, the *Yalobusha Review*, *Heather McHugh's New Voices 1989–1998 from The Academy of American Poets*, and elsewhere.

CYNTHIA LOWEN is a graduate of Sarah Lawrence College's MFA in Creative Writing Program and an editor at Four Way Books. She is a recipient of a fellowship to the Fine Arts Work Center in Provincetown, Massachusetts, as well as the Discovery/*Boston Review* Prize, the Campbell Corner Prize, the *Tin House*/Summer Literary Seminars Kenya Prize, and the *Inkwell* 11th Annual Poetry Prize, among others. Her work has appeared in *Barrow Street*, *Black Warrior Review*, *Boston Review*, *Inkwell*, the *Laurel Review*, *Lumina*, and *Provincetown Arts*, among others. She lives in New York City.

DENIS MAIR's translations from Chinese include memoirs by the Buddhist monk Shih Chen-hua, an autobiography by the philosopher Feng Youlan, and fiction by China's former Minister of Culture

Wang Meng. He has taught college courses on the *I Ching* and Chinese poetry.

IONA MAN-CHEONG's translations (in collaboration with Eliot Weinberger) include *Unlock: Poems by Bei Dao* and the poems of Ni Ruixuan in *Women Writers of Traditional China: An Anthology of Poetry and Criticism*.

CATE MARVIN is the author of two poetry collections, *World's Tallest Disaster* (2001) and *Fragment of the Head of a Queen* (2007), and coeditor with the poet Michael Dumanis of the anthology *Legitimate Dangers* (2006), all of which were published by Sarabande Books. She is the recipient of the Kathryn A. Morton Prize, the Kate Tufts Discovery Prize, and a Whiting Award. She is presently an associate professor in creative writing at the College of Staten Island, City University of New York.

GARDNER MCFALL is the author of *The Pilot's Daughter* and a forthcoming second collection of poems, *Russian Tortoise*. New work is scheduled to appear in *River Styx*, the *Sewanee Review*, *Poet Lore*, and the Alhambra Poetry Calendar 2009. She teaches at Hunter College in New York City.

PABLO MEDINA is the author of eleven books, among them *Points of Balance/Puntos de apoyo* and *The Cigar Roller*. In January 2008, Medina and fellow poet Mark Statman published a new English version of García Lorca's *Poet in New York*. Medina is on the faculty of the Warren Wilson MFA Program for Writers in Asheville, North Carolina, and is professor of English at the University of Nevada, Las Vegas. He was on the board of AWP, serving as board president in 2005–06.

CHRISTOPHER MERRILL has published four collections of poetry, including *Brilliant Water* and *Watch Fire*, for which he received the Peter I. B. Lavan Younger Poets Award from the Academy of American Poets; translations of Aleš Debeljak's *Anxious Moments* and *The City and the Child*; several edited volumes, among them, *The Forgotten Language: Contemporary Poets and Nature* and *From the Faraway Nearby: Georgia O'Keeffe as Icon*; and four books of nonfiction, *The Grass of Another Country: A Journey*

Through the World of Soccer, The Old Bridge: The Third Balkan War and the Age of the Refugee, Only the Nails Remain: Scenes from the Balkan Wars, and *Things of the Hidden God: Journey to the Holy Mountain*. His work has been translated into twenty-five languages, his journalism appears in many publications, and he is the book critic for the daily radio news program *The World*. He has held the William H. Jenks Chair in Contemporary Letters at the College of the Holy Cross and now directs the International Writing Program at the University of Iowa.

TEDI LÓPEZ MILLS is a poet, essayist, translator, and editor. From 1994 to 1999, she was editor in chief of the literary journal *La Gaceta*. In 1998, she received the first poetry grant awarded by the Octavio Paz Foundation. Her poetry books include *Cinco estaciones, Un lugar ajeno, Segunda persona* (for which she received the Efraín Huerta National Literature Prize), *Glosas, Horas*, and *Luz por aire y agua*. A small selection of her work has just been published by Kore Press, under the title While Light Is Built.

PAUL MULDOON's main collections of poetry are *New Weather* (1973); *Mules* (1977); *Why Brownlee Left* (1980); *Quoof* (1983); *Meeting The British* (1987); *Madoc: A Mystery* (1990); *The Annals of Chile* (1994); *Hay* (1998); *Poems 1968–1998* (2001); and *Moy Sand and Gravel* (2002), for which he won the 2003 Pulitzer Prize. His tenth collection, *Horse Latitudes*, appeared in the fall of 2006.

LES MURRAY was born October 17, 1938, in Bunyah, New South Wales, Australia. His recent collections include *The Biplane Houses* (2007); *Poems the Size of Photographs* (2004); *Learning Human: Selected Poems* (1998), which was shortlisted for the International Griffin Poetry Prize; and *Subhuman Redneck Poems*, winner of the 1996 T. S. Eliot Prize. His many awards include the Queens Gold Medal for Poetry, awarded to him in 1999. He is also the author of two verse novels: *The Boys Who Stole the Funeral* (1992) and *Fredy Neptune: A Novel in Verse* (1999). He was formerly the editor of *Poetry Australia* and is currently the editor of *Quadrant* magazine. He resides in his native Bunyah.

Born Ricardo Eliecer Neftalí Reyes Basoalto in southern Chile on July 12, 1904, PABLO NERUDA led a life charged with poetic and political activity. In 1923 he sold all of his possessions to finance the publication of his first book, *Crepusculario* (*Twilight*). He published the volume under the pseudonym "Pablo Neruda" to avoid conflict with his family, who disapproved of his occupation. The following year, he found a publisher for *Veinte poemas de amor y una cancion desesperada* (*Twenty Love Poems and a Song of Despair*). The book made a celebrity of Neruda. In 1927, he began his long career as a diplomat in the Latin American tradition of honoring poets with diplomatic assignments. Upon returning to Chile in 1943, he was elected to the senate and joined the Communist Party. When the Chilean government moved to the right, they declared communism illegal and expelled Neruda from the senate. He went into hiding. During those years he wrote and published *Canto general* (1950). In 1952 the government withdrew the order to arrest leftist writers and political figures, and Neruda returned to Chile. For the next twenty-one years, he continued a career that integrated private and public concerns and became known as the people's poet. Neruda received numerous prestigious awards, including the International Peace Prize in 1950, the Lenin Peace Prize and the Stalin Peace Prize in 1953, and the Nobel Prize for Literature in 1971. Neruda died of leukemia on September 23, 1973.

AIMEE NEZHUKUMATATHIL is the author of *At the Drive-In Volcano* (2007), winner of the Balcones Prize, and *Miracle Fruit* (2003), winner of the *ForeWord Magazine* Poetry Book of the Year and the Global Filipino Literary Award. New poems appear in *Antioch Review*, *FIELD*, and *American Poetry Review*. She is an associate professor of English at SUNY-Fredonia, where she was awarded a Chancellor's Medal of Excellence.

MIHO NONAKA is a bilingual writer born and raised in Tokyo. Her first book of Japanese poems, *Garasu no tsuki*, was a finalist for Japan's national poetry prize. Her poems and nonfiction in English have appeared or are forthcoming in *Quarterly West*, *Crab Orchard Review*, *Prairie Schooner*, *Iowa Review*, and *The Spoon River Poetry Review*, among others. She is an associate professor of English at Eastern Illinois University.

DENNIS NURKSE's collections include *Voices Over Water, Leaving Xaia,* and *The Rules of Paradise,* published by Four Way books, as well as the new collection *The Border Kingdom.* He has taught workshops at Rikers Island, and his poems about prison life appear in *American Poetry Review,* the *New Yorker,* the *Paris Review, TriQuarterly,* the *Kenyon Review,* and other magazines. He also translates anonymous medieval and flamenco Spanish lyric poems. He has taught at the New School, Columbia University, and Sarah Lawrence College.

ED OCHESTER's most recent books are *Unreconstructed: Poems Selected and New* (2007); the chapbook *The Republic of Lies* (2007); *The Land of Cockaigne* (2001); and *American Poetry Now* (2007), an anthology of contemporary American poetry. He edits the Pitt Poetry Series and is general editor of the Drue Heinz Literature Prize for short fiction. He has won fellowships from the National Endowment for the Arts and the Pennsylvania Council on the Arts and recently won the Artist of the Year Award of the Pittsburgh Cultural Trust. He coedits the poetry magazine 5 AM and is a core faculty member of the Bennington College MFA program.

SHARON OLDS's first collection of poems, *Satan Says* (1980), received the inaugural San Francisco Poetry Center Award. Olds's following collection, *The Dead & the Living* (1983), received the Lamont Poetry Selection in 1983 and the National Book Critics Circle Award. Her other collections include *Strike Sparks: Selected Poems* (2004); *The Unswept Room* (2002); *Blood, Tin, Straw* (1999); *The Gold Cell* (1997); *The Wellspring* (1995); and *The Father* (1992), which was shortlisted for the T. S. Eliot Prize and was a finalist for the National Book Critics Circle Award. Olds's numerous honors include a National Endowment for the Arts grant and a Guggenheim Foundation Fellowship. Her poetry has appeared in the *New Yorker,* the *Paris Review,* and *Ploughshares* and has been anthologized in more than one hundred collections. Olds held the position of New York State Poet from 1998 to 2000.

DIANA PARK is currently a Fulbright fellow in South Korea. She dislikes brown tree snakes because of what happened to the birds on Guam.

CECILY PARKS is the author of *Field Folly Snow* (University of Georgia Press/VQR Poetry Series, 2008) and the chapbook *Cold Work* (Poetry Society of America, 2005). She is a PhD candidate in English at the CUNY Graduate Center.

VERA PAVLOVA was born in 1963, in Moscow. Up to the age of eighteen she studied to become a composer and began writing poetry at the age of twenty. The first selection of her published poetry appeared in the journal *Yunost*. Her first collection was released in 1997, followed by five other collections, the last containing 800 poems, written over a period of eighteen years. Pavlova became a celebrity after the publication of over seventy-two poems in the paper *Segodnia* (with a postscript by Boris Kuzminsky), which gave rise to the rumor that she was a literary hoax. Her poetry has been translated into over fifteen languages.

CATE PEEBLES has lived in Pittsburgh, Portland, and Paris, and she currently resides in Brooklyn. Her poetry can be found in print and on the Web in such journals as *Octopus*, *La Petite Zine*, *Cannibal*, *CutBank*, and elsewhere. She coedits the journal *Fou* (www.foumagazine.net).

LUCIA PERILLO's fourth book of poems, *Luck is Luck*, was a finalist for the *L.A. Times* Book Prize and was awarded the Kingsley Tufts Prize from Claremont University. Her poetry and prose also earned her a MacArthur Fellowship in 2000. A book of her essays, *I've Heard the Vultures Singing*, was published by Trinity University Press in 2007. Her new book of poems, *Inseminating the Elephant*, will be published in 2009 by Copper Canyon.

CARL PHILLIPS is the author of ten books of poetry, most recently *Quiver of Arrows: Selected Poems 1986–2006* and *Speak Low*, forthcoming in the spring of 2009. He teaches at Washington University in St. Louis.

D. A. POWELL's collections include *Tea, Lunch, Cocktails* and *Chronic*. A bilingual English/German edition of his selected poems is also available from Lux Books. Powell's work has appeared recently in *The Best*

American Poetry, *Kenyon Review*, *Quarterly West*, and *Boulevard*. He teaches in the English Department of the University of San Francisco.

LIA PURPURA's collection of essays, *On Looking* (2006), was a finalist for the National Book Critics Circle Award in 2007. *King Baby: Poems* won the Beatrice Hawley Award from Alice James Books in 2008. Purpura is also the author of *Increase* (winner of the AWP Award in Creative Nonfiction); *Stone Sky Lifting* (winner of the Ohio State University Press Award); and *The Brighter the Veil*. The recipient of NEA and Fulbright fellowships, her work has appeared in *Agni*, *DoubleTake*, *Field*, *Georgia Review*, *Iowa Review*, *Orion*, *Parnassus: Poetry in Review*, *Ploughshares*, *Southern Review*, and elsewhere. She is writer-in-residence at Loyola College in Baltimore, Maryland.

BIN RAMKE has written nine poetry collections, including *Wake*, *The Erotic Light of Gardens*, *The Language Student*, and *Tendril*. He was awarded the Yale Younger Poets Award in 1978 and has since won the Pushcart Prize four times and the Iowa Poetry Prize twice.

JESSICA REED's poetry has appeared in the *Paris Review*, *Lit*, and The Huffington Post, as well as in various online journals. She is the 2007 recipient of the Marie Ponsot Poetry Prize and the Jerome Lowell Dejur Award. Originally from Asheville, North Carolina, she lives in New York City, where she spends M−F/9−5 as a technical writer and where she received her MFA from the City College of New York in 2008.

PAISLEY REKDAL is the author of a book of essays, *The Night My Mother Met Bruce Lee* (Pantheon, October 2000 and Vintage Books, April 2002), and three books of poetry, *A Crash of Rhinos* (2000); *Six Girls Without Pants* (2002); and *The Invention of the Kaleidoscope* (2007). Her work has received a *Village Voice* Writers on the Verge Award, an NEA Fellowship, the University of Georgia Press's Contemporary Poetry Series Award, a Fulbright Fellowship, several Pushcart Prize nominations, and the Laurence Goldstein Poetry Prize from *Michigan Quarterly Review*. Her poems and essays have appeared in or are forthcoming from the *New York Times Magazine*, NPR, *Ploughshares*, *Poetry*, *Black Warrior*

Review, *New England Review*, *Virginia Quarterly Review*, *Kenyon Review*, and *American Poetry Review*, among other publications.

MAGGIE ROBBINS, a student of psychoanalysis in her hometown of New York City, is the author of *Suzy Zeus Gets Organized*, a novel in verse. Her essay "How I Know What I Know" was anthologized in last year's *Heaven*, from Church Publishing. She is fluent in Swahili and can be contacted at mrobbins99@earthlink.net.

ROBIN ROBERTSON's first poetry collection, *A Painted Field*, won the 1997 Forward Prize for Best First Collection and the Scottish First Book of the Year Award. His second collection, *Slow Air*, appeared in 2002. His third collection, *Swithering*, was published in 2006 and won the 2006 Forward Prize for Best Collection and was shortlisted for the T. S. Eliot Prize. Robertson's poetry appears regularly in the *London Review of Books*, *Poetry*, and the *New Yorker*. In 2004, Robertson received the E. M. Forster Award from the American Academy of Arts and Letters.

PATTIANN ROGERS has published thirteen books, the most recent, *Wayfare*, from Penguin in 2008. Her poetry has received several awards, including a Guggenheim Fellowship, two NEA grants, a Literary Award from the Lannan Foundation in 2005, and five Pushcart Prizes. Her papers are archived in the Sowell Collection at Texas Tech University. She has two sons and three grandsons and lives with her husband in Colorado.

MARY RUEFLE is the author of ten books of poetry, most recently *Indeed I Was Pleased With the World* (Carnegie Mellon, 2007). A book of short fiction, *The Most Of It*, was published by Wave Books in 2008. Her poems and prose appear in many anthologies, including *The Best American Poetry*, *Great American Prose Poems*, and *The Next American Essay*. She lives in southern Vermont.

TOMAŽ ŠALAMUN is a Slovenian poet, born in 1941 in Zagreb, Croatia, and considered to be one of the great postwar Central European poets. Šalamun has taught at the Universities of Alabama, Tennessee,

Georgia, Massachusetts, Pittsburgh, and Richmond and was invited to be a member of the International Writing Program at the University of Iowa in 1971. He spent several years as cultural attaché to the Slovenian consulate in New York. His books have been translated into nineteen languages and nine of his thirty-seven books of poetry have been published in English, including *The Book for My Brother* (2006); *Poker* (2003, 2008); *Row* (2006); and *Woods and Chalices* (2008). In 2007, Šalamun received the European Prize in Münster in Germany. His *There's the Hand and There's the Arid Chair*, translated by Thomas Kane, is due out by Counterpath Press in 2009.

CHRISTOPHER SCHMIDT is the author of a book of poems, *The Next in Line* (Slope Editions, 2008). He teaches at Brooklyn College and Bard College.

STEVEN SEYMOUR is a professional interpreter/translator who worked for years on contract to the U.S. Department of State. He interpreted at the Geneva Disarmament Talks in the seventies and eighties and served at the U.S. Embassy in Moscow in the nineties. In addition to Russian, he has worked in Polish, French, and Spanish.

JASON SHINDER (1955–2008) was the author of three poetry collections, including *Stupid Hope*, forthcoming from Graywolf Press, and *Among Women* and the editor of numerous anthologies, including *The Poem That Changed America: "Howl" Fifty Years Later*. He directed the YMCA National Writer's Voice and taught at the Writing Seminars at Bennington College.

LORI SHINE's poems have appeared in *6x6*, *American Poetry Review*, *Boston Review*, *Conduit*, *New American Writing*, and other magazines and in the anthology *Isn't It Romantic: 100 Love Poems by Younger American Poets*. A chapbook, *Coming Down in White*, was published by Pilot Books. She lives in Easthampton, Massachusetts.

ELENI SIKELIANOS is the author of seven books, including *Body Clock* and *The Book of Jon*. Her translation of Jacques Roubaud's *Exchanges on Light* will soon be out from La Presse. Over the years, she has received a number of awards for her poetry, nonfiction, and translations, among them a National Endowment for the Arts Award, a Fulbright Senior Scholar Writing Fellowship, the National Poetry Series Award, and two Gertrude Stein Awards for Innovative American Writing. She shares her days with the novelist Laird Hunt and their daughter, Eva Grace, and teaches in and directs the Creative Writing Program at the University of Denver.

CHARLES SIMIC was born on May 9, 1938, in Belgrade, Yugoslavia. His first full-length collection of poems, *What the Grass Says*, was published in 1967. Since then he has published more than sixty books in the United States and abroad, twenty titles of his own poetry among them, including *That Little Something* (2008); *My Noiseless Entourage* (2005); *Selected Poems: 1963–2003* (2004), for which he received the 2005 International Griffin Poetry Prize; *The Voice at 3:00 AM: Selected Late and New Poems* (2003); *Night Picnic* (2001); *The Book of Gods and Devils* (2000); *Jackstraws* (1999), which was named a Notable Book of the Year by the *New York Times*; *Walking the Black Cat* (1996), which was a finalist for the National Book Award; *A Wedding in Hell* (1994); *Hotel Insomnia* (1992); *The World Doesn't End: Prose Poems* (1990), for which he received the Pulitzer Prize for Poetry; *Selected Poems: 1963–1983* (1990); and *Unending Blues* (1986). Simic has received numerous awards, including fellowships from the Guggenheim Foundation, the MacArthur Foundation, and the National Endowment for the Arts, and was elected to the American Academy of Arts and Letters in 1995. Most recently, he was announced the recipient of the 2007 Wallace Stevens Award by the Academy of American Poets. Simic is Emeritus Professor at the University of New Hampshire, where he has taught since 1973.

BRUCE SMITH was born and raised in Philadelphia, Pennsylvania. He is the author of five books of poems: *The Common Wages*; *Silver and Information* (National Poetry Series, selected by Hayden Carruth); *Mercy Seat*; *The Other Lover* (University of Chicago), which was a finalist for both the National Book Award and the Pulitzer Prize; and, most recently, *Songs for Two Voices* (Chicago, 2005). He teaches at Syracuse University.

CHARLIE SMITH is the author of seven poetry books, including *Heroin*, *Women of America*, and the forthcoming *Word Comix*, and nine novels and novellas, including the forthcoming *Three Delays* and *You Are Welcome Here*. He's won numerous awards, grants, and fellowships, including Guggenheim, NEA, and New York Foundation for the Arts grants and the Levinson Prize for Poetry and the Aga Khan Prize from the *Paris Review*. Five of his books were *New York Times* Notable Books. He has taught at Iowa and Princeton and was Coal Royalty Chairholder at the University of Alabama. He lives in New York City.

MARK STATMAN's writing has appeared in numerous publications, including *Tin House*, *Subtropics*, *Hanging Loose*, *Live Mag*, *The Hat*, *Upstreet*, *Bayou*, *Pingpong*, *The Duplications*, *conduit*, *Florida Review*, and *American Poetry Review*. His work has been featured on *Poetry Daily*, *The Bob Edwards Show*, *The Leonard Lopate Show*, and *New York Voices* (WNET-NY). He is the author of *Listener in the Snow* and, with Christian McEwen, edited *The Alphabet of the Trees: A Guide to Nature Writing*, and his essays and translations have appeared in eight other collections. With Pablo Medina, he translated Federico García Lorca's *Poet in New York* (Grove, 2008) and is currently working on a selection of translations of the poems of Jose María Hinojosa. A recipient of awards from the National Endowment for the Arts and the National Writers Project, Statman is an associate professor of literary studies at Eugene Lang College of the New School.

ALISON STINE's first book *Ohio Violence* won the Vassar Miller Prize, selected by Eric Pankey, and will be published by the University of North Texas Press in spring 2009. A former Wallace Stegner Fellow at Stanford University, she is also the author of a chapbook, *Lot of My Sister*, winner of the Wick Prize (Kent State University Press).

TERESE SVOBODA has published ten books of prose and poetry, including *Black Glasses Like Clark Kent*, winner of the Graywolf Nonfiction Prize. Her fifth book of poetry, *Weapons Grade*, and her fifth novel, *Pirate Talk or Mermelade*, will be published in 2009 and 2010. This spring she taught at Davidson College as the McGhee Professor in fiction and most recently taught poetry for the Summer Literary Seminars in Kenya.

WISLAWA SZYMBORSKA was born in Bnin (now a part of Kórnik) in Western Poland in 1923. She has published more than fifteen books of poetry, including *Widok z ziarnkiem piasku, 102 wiersze* (1996); *Ludzie na moscie* (1986); *Poezje wybrane II* (1983); *Wybór wierszy* (1973); *Poezje* (1970); *Poezje wybrane* (1967); and *Wolanie do Yeti* (1957). Her poems have been translated into many languages; her collections available in English include *Miracle Fair: Selected Poems of Wislawa Szymborska* (2001); *View with a Grain of Sand: Selected Poems* (1995); *People on a Bridge* (1990); and *Sounds, Feelings, Thoughts: Seventy Poems* (1981). Among her many honors and awards are a Goethe Prize, a Herder Prize, and a Polish PEN Club Prize.

JAMES TATE's first collection of poems, *The Lost Pilot* (1967), was selected by Dudley Fitts for the Yale Series of Younger Poets while Tate was a still student at the University of Iowa Writers' Workshop, making him one of the youngest poets to receive the honor. He has published several collections of poems, most recently *The Ghost Soldiers* (2008); *Return to the City of White Donkeys* (2004); *Memoir of the Hawk* (2001); *Shroud of the Gnome* (1997); and *Worshipful Company of Fletchers* (1994), which won the National Book Award. He served as editor of *The Best American Poetry 1997*. Tate's honors include a National Institute of Arts and Letters Award for Poetry, the Wallace Stevens Award, a 1995 Tanning Prize, and fellowships from the Guggenheim Foundation and the National Endowment for the Arts.

DANIEL TIFFANY is the author of *Puppet Wardrobe* (Free Verse Editions); *Toy Medium: Materialism and Modern Lyric* (University of California Press); and *Radio Corpse: Imagism and the Cryptaesthetic of Ezra Pound*.

QUINCY TROUPE is the former poet laureate of California and the author of seventeen books, including eight volumes of poetry. Troupe has received two American Book Awards, one for a collection of poetry, *Snake-Back Solos*, and the other for *Miles: The Autobiography*, coauthored with Miles Davis. A film (for which Troupe wrote the screenplay) based on his book *Miles and Me*, a memoir of his friendship with Miles Davis, is scheduled for release in theaters in fall 2009. Coffee House Press published his newest volume of poems, *The Architecture of*

Language, the recipient of the 2007 Patterson Award for Sustained Literary Excellence, in October 2006. His previous collection of poetry, *Transcircularities: New and Selected Poems*, won the 2003 Milt Kessler Poetry Award and was selected by *Publishers Weekly* as one of the ten best books of poetry published in 2002. Professor Emeritus at the University of California, San Diego, Troupe is editor of *Black Renaissance Noire*, a journal of academic writing, culture, literature, politics, music, and visual arts published by the Institute of African American Affairs at New York University. He lives in New York City.

Born in Poznan, Poland, JOANNA TRZECIAK has been Wislawa Szymborska's authorized translator since 1989. Her translations have appeared in the *New Yorker* and the *New York Times*. Other translation projects include the short stories of Stanislaw Lem and a novel by Tomek Tryzna.

CHASE TWICHELL's books of poetry include *The Snow Watcher* (1998); *The Ghost of Eden* (1995); *Perdido* (1991); *The Odds* (1986); and *Northern Spy* (1981). She has won awards from the Artists Foundation (Boston), the New Jersey State Council on the Arts, and the American Academy of Arts and Letters and fellowships from the Guggenheim Foundation and the National Endowment for the Arts. From 1976 to 1984 she worked at Pennyroyal Press, and from 1986 to 1988 she coedited the Alabama Poetry Series, published by the University of Alabama Press. She also coedited *The Practice of Poetry: Writing Exercises from Poets Who Teach* (1992) with Robin Behn. She has taught at Princeton University, Goddard College, Warren Wilson College, the University of Alabama, and Hampshire College. In 1999 Twichell founded Ausable Press.

MUKOMA WA NGUGI is the author of *Hurling Words at Consciousness* (poems, 2006), and *Conversing with Africa: Politics of Change* (2003) and editor of the forthcoming anthology *New Kenyan Fiction* (Ishmael Reed Publications). In addition to his political essays and columns appearing in the *International Herald Tribune*, *Progressive Magazine*, the *Los Angeles Times*, the *Christian Science Monitor*, *Radical History Review*, *Monthly Review*, the *Progressive*, and the *Mail and Guardian*, his writing has also appeared in the *New York Quarterly*, *Brick*, *Kwani?*, *Chimurenga*, and *Wasafiri*. He is a political columnist for the BBC *Focus on Africa* magazine and has forthcoming work in the *Kenyon Review*.

ELIOT WEINBERGER is the primary translator of Octavio Paz into English. His anthology *American Poetry Since 1950: Innovators and Outsiders* (1993) was a best-seller in Mexico, and his edition of Jorge Luis Borges's *Selected Non-Fictions* (1999) received the National Book Critics Circle prize for criticism. In 1992, he was given PEN's first Gregory Kolovakos Award for his work in promoting Hispanic literature in the United States, and in 2000 he was the first American literary writer to be awarded the Order of the Aztec Eagle by the government of Mexico. Weinberger's recent publications are the collection of essays *Karmic Traces: 1993–1999* and a translation of Bei Dao's *Unlock* (with Iona Man-Cheong), both published by New Directions in 2000. He is the editor of *The New Directions Anthology of Classical Chinese Poetry* (2003).

JILLIAN WEISE wrote *The Amputee's Guide to Sex* (Soft Skull Press) and *Translating the Body* (All Nations Press). She is an assistant professor at Clemson. Soon she will be in Patagonia on a creative writing Fulbright.

WILLIAM WENTHE's books of poems are *Not Till We Are Lost* (LSU Press) and *Birds of Hoboken* (Orchises Press). Among his awards are Pushcart Prizes and an NEA fellowship. He teaches creative writing and modern poetry at Texas Tech University.

C. K. WILLIAMS is the author of numerous books of poetry, including *The Singing* (2004), which won the National Book Award; *Repair* (1999), winner of a Pulitzer Prize; *The Vigil* (1997); *A Dream of Mind* (1992); *Flesh and Blood* (1987), which won the National Book Critics Circle Award; *Tar* (1983); *With Ignorance* (1997); *I Am the Bitter Name* (1992); and *Lies* (1969). Among his many awards and honors are an American Academy of Arts and Letters Award, a Guggenheim Fellowship, the Lila Wallace-Reader's Digest Award, the PEN/Voelcker Award for Poetry, and a Pushcart Prize.

MONICA YOUN is the author of *Barter* (Graywolf Press, 2003). She has been awarded a 2008 Witter Bynner Poetry Fellowship from the Library of Congress and a 2008 Bellagio residency from the Rockefeller Foundation, as well as a Wallace Stegner Fellowship from Stanford University. She is an attorney at the Brennan Center for Justice at NYU School of Law, focusing on election law and campaign finance reform issues, and has taught creative writing at Columbia University and Pratt Institute.

DEAN YOUNG is the William Livingston Chair of Poetry at the University of Texas at Austin. His most recent book is *Primitive Mentor*.

Poet, novelist, essayist ADAM ZAGAJEWSKI was born in Lwów in 1945. He first became well known as one of the leading poets of the Generation of '68 or the Polish New Wave (Nowa fala); he is one of Poland's most famous contemporary poets. Among his collections are *Pragnienie* (1999); *Ziemia ognista* (1994); *Jechac do Lwowa* (1985); *Sklepy miesne* (1975); and *Komunikat* (1972). He is also the author of a memoir, *Another Beauty* (2000, translated by Clare Cavanagh), and the prose collections *Two Cities* (1995, translated by Lillian Vallee) and *Solitude and Solidarity* (1990, translated by Lillian Vallee). His poems and essays have been translated into many languages. Among his honors and awards are a fellowship from the Berliner Kunstlerprogramm, the Kurt Tucholsky Prize, a Prix de la Liberté, and a Guggenheim Fellowship.

JASON ZUZGA's poetry has been published in journals such as *Fence*, *jubilat*, *Volt*, *Lit*, the *Yale Review*, *Gulf Coast*, *Spork*, and *Fulcrum*. He was a winter poetry fellow at the Fine Arts Work Center in Provincetown in 2001–02 and the James Merrill Writer-in-Residence in Stongington, Connecticut, from September 2005 to August 2006.

COPYRIGHT NOTES AND PERMISSIONS